Broken Promises

Northeastern University 1898–1998

The Northeastern Series on
WHITE-COLLAR AND ORGANIZATIONAL CRIME
edited by Kip Schlegel and David Weisburd

BROKEN PROMISES

Fraud by Small Business Health Insurers

ROBERT TILLMAN

Northeastern University Press / Boston

NORTHEASTERN UNIVERSITY PRESS

Copyright 1998 by Robert Tillman

Library of Congress Cataloging-in-Publication Data

Tillman, Robert.
    Broken promises : fraud by small business health insurers / Robert Tillman.
        p.   cm. — (Northeastern series on white-collar and organizational crime)
    Includes bibliographical references and index.
        ISBN 1–55553–376–0 (cloth   :   alk. paper). — ISBN 1–55553–375–2 (pbk. : alk. paper)
        i. Insurance crimes—United States.   2. Insurance, Health—Corrupt practices—United States.   3. Self–employed—Crimes against—United States.   4. Small business—Employees—Crimes against—United States.   I. Title.   II. Series.
    HV6769.T55   1998
    364.16'3—dc21   98–23539

Supported under award #95-IJ-CX-0030 from the National Institute of Justice, Office of Justice Programs, U.S. Department of Justice. Points of view in this document are those of the author and do not necessarily represent the official position of the U.S. Department of Justice.

Designed by Christopher Kuntze

Composed in Sabon by G&S Typesetters, Inc., in Austin, Texas. Printed and bound by Edwards Brothers, Inc., in Lillington, North Carolina. The paper is Glatfelter, an acid-free sheet.

Manufactured in the United States of America

02 01 00 99 98   5 4 3 2 1

Contents

Abbreviations

ABL	American Benefit Ltd. Trust
ABT	American Benefit Trust
AHBT	Atlantic Healthcare Benefits Trust
ASP	All Saints Program
ATG	Association of Trust and Guarantee
ATS	Alliance Temporary Services
AWF	American Workforce
BAT	Benefits Administrators Trust
CABE	California Association of Builders Exchange
CBN	Christian Brotherhood Newsletter
CREATE	Council for Recreation, Energy, and Tourist Enrichment
DHC	Diversified Health Concepts
DOL	U.S. Department of Labor
ERIC	ERISA Industry Committee
ERISA	Employee Retirement Income Security Act
ERS	Employment Resource Services
GAO	General Accounting Office
HMO	health maintenance organization
IAEA	International Association of Entrepreneurs of America
IFF	International Forum of Florida
IPCMEA	International Professional, Craft and Maintenance Employees Association

IPCMEU	International Professional, Craft and Maintenance Employees Union
IUPA	International Union of Police Associations
MBT	Ministers Benefit Trust
MET	multiple employer trust
MEWA	multiple employer welfare arrangement
MSA	medical savings account
NAM	National Association of Manufacturers
NAPE	National Association of Professionals and Executives
NCAE	National Council of Allied Employees
NCCMP	National Coordinating Committee for Multiemployer Plans
NETA	National Employers Trade Association
NFBA	National Family Business Association
NIC	National Insurance Consultants
NICB	National Insurance Crime Bureau
NSA	National Staff Alliance
OIG	Office of the Inspector General
OLR	Office of Labor Racketeering
PAI	Progressive Administrators Inc.
PEAA	Professional Employees and Affiliates Association
PPO	preferred provider organization
PWBA	Pension and Welfare Benefits Administration
RHIS	Rubell-Helm Insurance Services
USF&G	United States Financial and Guarantee Association
WBA	Western Businessmen's Association

Broken Promises

Introduction

IN late 1989, John and Louise Rayfield faced a serious
problem.[1] Like millions of Americans this middle-aged,
self-employed California couple desperately needed affordable health insurance. The monthly premiums for the
policy they'd had since 1985 had increased to the point where
they could no longer afford it. But they also knew how difficult
it would be to find another company willing to issue them a
policy because they had numerous medical problems that included eye, heart, pancreas, and gall bladder conditions (what
insurance companies call *preexisting conditions*), all of which
required ongoing treatment. Their dilemma seemed to be resolved when an insurance agent told them of a new plan being offered by New York–based Empire Blue Cross that was
both considerably less expensive than their current policy and
would cover all of their preexisting conditions. In January
1990, the Rayfields canceled their existing health insurance
policy and signed up with Empire. Only later did they learn
that, despite the fact that they were self-employed, they had
become members of a labor union, Local 867, and that their
health plan was actually being offered through something
called the Consolidated Welfare Fund.

3

After diligently paying their monthly premiums, in September 1990, just nine months after they had enrolled in the plan, the Rayfields were informed that their coverage with Empire/Consolidated had been terminated retroactively, but they were eligible to enroll in a new program. Over the next year and a half, they found themselves being bounced from one plan to another, first to an organization called the National Association of Professionals and Executives (NAPE) and then to an offshore insurance company called Winston-Hill. In December 1991, their agent informed them that they would thereafter receive health insurance coverage from the Old American Insurance Company through something called the Western Businessmen's Association. All the while, their insurance agent assured the Rayfields that their medical expenses would be covered.

He lied. Over the 2-year period after they signed with Empire, the Rayfields suffered a number of health problems that required extensive treatment, resulting in medical bills that totaled over $88,000. By March 1992, the Rayfields realized that their claims were not being paid, nor would they ever be paid.

More than simply facing overwhelming medical bills, the Rayfields suffered physical harm as a result of their unwitting participation in an insurance scam. When they learned that their claims would not be covered, they stopped seeking treatments for their various medical conditions. As a result, those conditions worsened. Mrs. Rayfield needed a cornea transplant at a cost of $50,000. Because she could not afford to pay for the operation, she was forced to live with blurred vision for the rest of her life.

The Rayfields later learned that they were not alone. Thousands of people, most of whom were either self-employed or worked for small companies and made relatively low wages, had been ripped off by a nationwide ring of insurance crooks. When the victims reported their experiences to state insurance departments that regulated insurance companies, they learned that the agencies had no jurisdiction over the organizations that sold them the worthless policies. Because these groups were not licensed insurance companies, there was nothing the regulatory agencies could do.

THE CRIMINOGENIC INDUSTRY

This book is about white-collar criminals in the health insurance industry and the schemes they perpetrate on people like the Rayfields. These are complicated crimes that involve organized networks of criminals that operate nationally and internationally and are amazingly resistant to law enforcement agencies' efforts to stop them. These criminal organizations and their schemes are described in some detail in this book. Yet to fully understand the plight of people like the Rayfields, one has to look beyond the individual criminals involved and examine the environment in which they operate. Specifically, one has to examine the broader market conditions that create a demand for the insurance crooks' products as well as the regulatory laws and agencies that allow these "financial knaves and buccaneers" (as one regulator called them) to operate with near impunity.[2] These too are described here.

The insurance industry is particularly vulnerable to fraud and abuse. Unlike other industries that produce tangible products or provide immediate services to customers, the business of insurance essentially involves the *selling of promises*— "promise(s) to pay all or a part of the costs associated with some future event."[3] In some cases the consumer may rarely use the services being paid for. Moreover, transactions in the industry are characterized by a *long tail;* that is, a long period of time often elapses between the date when a customer begins paying for future services (coverage of health care costs) and the date that those services are actually demanded (when a claim is filed).[4] In the interim, unscrupulous insurance company owners and operators have ample time to abscond with their clients' premiums. Thus, by its very nature, the insurance industry provides an ideal vehicle for financial fraud.

The crimes described in this book take place in the small business or small group health insurance industry—the industry that supplies health insurance to the employees of small companies and to self-employed individuals. The victims are gas station attendants, beauticians, construction workers, waiters, farm workers, and other employees of small businesses whose wages are relatively low and who cannot afford to purchase individual health insurance policies. In recent years, the small business health insurance industry has been transformed into what criminologists refer to as a *criminogenic industry,* one whose very structure facilitates and encourages fraud and abuse within its ranks. How this transformation took place is an important part of the story, for it was these changes that created the structural conditions that made these white-collar crimes possible.

Chapter 2 describes these structural changes in more detail, but to set the stage, here is a brief summary. The wave of fraud in the small business health insurance industry that began in the late 1970s and continues to this day has its roots in two broad structural changes that affected the availability of health insurance in the United States. First, the last 30 years or so have witnessed dramatic changes in the health insurance industry. During this period, most large insurance companies simply left the market altogether as many large corporations began to set up their own insurance plans and as health maintenance organizations (HMOs) and other managed care networks began to make significant inroads into the health care market. Particularly hard hit was the small group market, which, because of its inherent risks and low profitability, was all but abandoned by traditional insurance companies. Those companies that remained in the market sought to increase their profits by insuring only the "cream of the crop," those individuals who were relatively healthy and whose medical costs would be low. As a result of these trends, small business owners saw their health insurance costs rise dramatically, and many were unable to find insurance for their employees at any cost.

The second change provided the means for committing fraud in the small group market. In 1974, Congress passed the Employee Retirement Income Security Act (ERISA), the primary purpose of which was to safeguard employee pension plans. But buried within the law were important provisions that allowed noninsurance companies to market health insurance plans as "employee welfare benefits." Significantly, the law stated that such plans would not be subject to state regulations as licensed insurance companies are; neither would they be subject to any significant federal oversight. Thus, while ERISA's provisions were intended to make it easier for employers, labor unions, and other organizations to provide health benefits to employees, they had the unintended effect of opening the doors to con artists who saw in them the legal loopholes that would become the vehicles for massive fraud.

These two structural changes created an environment where demand for health benefits among small business employees was high and supply in the legitimate market was low, a situation in which white-collar criminals were able to thrive by creating what essentially constituted a black market in health insurance. The Rayfields were just two of the thousands of people who were unwitting participants in that black market.

HEALTH CARE FRAUD AND THE HEALTH INSURANCE CRISIS

As the cost of medical care has skyrocketed in recent years, so has the amount of money lost to fraud and abuse within the health care industry. Recent estimates suggest that this latter figure may be as high as $100 billion a year, or 10 percent of the $1 trillion spent on health care in the United States annually.[5] Every 19 months, Americans spend roughly $175 billion—the equivalent of what went to bail out the savings and loan industry in the 1980s—on health care fraud.[6]

Health care fraud takes three principal forms: (1) claimant fraud, committed by health care consumers; (2) provider

fraud, committed by physicians, laboratories, and other providers of health care services; and (3) insider fraud, committed
by individuals within the health insurance industry who use
their positions to divert money from insurance plans. To date,
the overwhelming focus in the public and private sectors has
been on the first two forms of health care fraud. However, one
could argue that insider fraud is more serious than the other
two forms. Few if any insurance companies have failed because of claimant or provider fraud. They simply pass the costs
on to the consumer. By contrast, when insiders create phony
insurance companies that inevitably go bankrupt because they
were never intended to pay off claims, thousands of individuals
who have diligently paid their premiums are often left with
staggering medical bills and, worse yet, may be unable to obtain health care coverage in the future. In a 1992 study, the
General Accounting Office (GAO, Congress's research arm)
estimated that between 1988 and 1991, a form of fraud in
the small business market involving what are known as *multiple employer welfare arrangements* (MEWAS) left more than
400,000 individuals with $133 million in unpaid medical
claims.[7]

Fraudulent insurance scams thrive in an environment where
many people are desperate to obtain medical coverage. Despite the fact that the U.S. health care system provides some of
the most technologically advanced medical treatments in the
world, an embarrassingly high proportion of American citizens find it difficult to obtain even basic medical care because
they cannot afford it. In 1996, some 17.4 percent of the nonelderly population, or 40.3 million Americans, had no health
insurance; of those, 9.8 million were children under the age of
18.[8] The consequences of being uninsured are serious. Studies
show that people who don't have health insurance often forgo
medical treatment, which in turn has a very adverse impact on
their health.[9]

Faced with such dire consequences, people turn to whatever
source they find available for affordable health insurance. As

one insurance regulator aptly put it, "If you're in quicksand and you're going down and all you see is a rotten limb, what is it you grab?"[10]

THE SOCIAL CONSTRUCTION OF INSURANCE FRAUD

If insider fraud in the health insurance industry is such a serious problem, why don't we hear more about it? Why do we more often hear news reports about individuals who file false workers' compensation claims, or who deliberately torch their own cars and then report them as stolen to collect the insurance money, or outrageous stories of individuals who jump on buses after they have crashed and claim they were injured in the accident? The answer lies in the way in which social problems are "socially constructed." In recent years, sociologists have focused on how what the public and policymakers define as social problems—those conditions that warrant some type of collective, often governmental, response—are often influenced by the media and by organized groups who hold some significant stake in having their claims about the existence of a certain problem accepted. Joseph Gusfield has eloquently argued that there exists a "culture of public problems" in which certain groups claim "ownership" of and "responsibility" for certain problems; inherent to these claims is a certain definition of the nature of the problem itself. Thus, for example, in the area of "drinking-driving," ownership and responsibility for the problem traditionally were claimed by an alliance of medical groups, government organizations, and insurance industry representatives who promoted a view of the problem that focused on the individual driver and his or her individual pathologies, primarily alcohol abuse. In this way other relevant factors, such as the safety features of automobiles and the conditions of highways, were excluded from consideration.[11]

In the area of insurance fraud the field has been dominated

by the insurance industry itself, which has clear-cut interests
in promoting a particular definition of the problem, one that
emphasizes the misconduct of claimants and providers but
downplays the significance of frauds committed by insurance
company owners and operators. In the United States, the regulation of the insurance industry has been left up to the individual states, many of which have created insurance commissions or departments. One of the duties of these agencies has
been to detect and investigate various forms of fraud within
the industry. As of 1996, some 28 states had created separate fraud bureaus within those agencies. Six of those states—
Arizona, California, Delaware, Maryland, Massachusetts,
and New Jersey—fund their fraud bureaus in part with as-
sessments on the insurance companies operating within the
states.[12] While this may be an expedient way to fund a government agency, it raises the possibility that the insurance companies will attempt to influence the focus of the bureaus they
fund. In California, the conflict between the interests of insurance companies and the broader goals of regulatory agencies
to protect consumers was so great that investigators within the
California Department of Insurance's fraud division filed a
lawsuit against heads of the agency claiming that, because of
the influence that insurers had on the agency's policies, they
were being forced to make criminal referrals on workers' compensation claims submitted to them by insurers without adequate review of the evidence.[13]

The insurance industry's definition of insurance fraud is
also promoted by private groups like the National Insurance
Crime Bureau (NICB). Established in 1992 by the merger of
two existing organizations, the National Automobile Theft
Bureau and the Insurance Crime Prevention Institute, the
NICB is funded largely by the insurance industry. With 200 of
its own investigators and large databases on stolen cars, the
organization provides investigative assistance to insurers and
law enforcement agencies. The NICB's view of the scope of insurance fraud is revealed in a brochure distributed as part of

its public awareness campaign. Described as an "insurance fraud overview," the brochure provides numerous examples of claimant fraud and provider fraud—from "staged accident rings" to doctors falsifying insurance claims—but never mentions insider insurance fraud.[14]

The insurance industry's view of insurance fraud does not preclude crimes by insurance company owners and insiders, it simply does not emphasize it. The industry's influence on both regulatory agencies and on policymakers results in relatively few public resources being expended on the investigation of insider insurance fraud, while large amounts of money are spent on claimant and provider fraud.

Federal law enforcement agencies focus their attention on frauds that directly affect the Medicare and Medicaid programs, often to the exclusion of other forms of fraud. In 1995, Louis Freeh, director of the Federal Bureau of Investigation (FBI), appeared before a congressional committee investigating trends in health care fraud. He told the committee that "health care fraud is a top national priority of the FBI" and that the agency's funding for health care fraud had increased from $31 million in 1991 to over $512 million in 1994. When asked what his agency was doing about frauds involving MEWAS and related health insurance scams, Freeh replied:

That's an area that we have not spent a lot of investigative time in, and I think that is because in health care fraud we're drawn to much more obviously notorious cases and cases that involve a little less expenditure of very scarce resources.[15]

Ironically, prior to assuming the head position at the FBI, Director Freeh had been a federal judge in New York where he presided over the early stages of a very large class action suit against the Consolidated Welfare Fund, an infamous health insurance provider that defrauded over 10,000 policyholders, including the Rayfields.[16]

THE ORIGINS OF
CRIMINOGENIC INDUSTRIES

One of the sociologically interesting things about small business health insurance fraud is that the origins of the problem seem so clearly rooted in the structure of the industry itself, suggesting strongly the industry's criminogenic nature. Before proceeding with the substantive discussion, it is useful to look more closely at the concept of criminogenic industries and to consider the question of how these industries emerge in the first place.

Research on white-collar crime shows that certain industries are more conducive to illegal conduct than others. In his classic 1930s analysis of what he termed *adverse decisions* against 70 large corporations, Edwin Sutherland found that certain industries, such as the meat packing industry, tended to have higher rates of legal violations than others.[17] In an analysis of criminal, civil, and regulatory violations among the 477 largest publicly owned manufacturing firms during the 1970s, Marshall Clinard and Peter Yeager found that violations were concentrated in the oil, automobile, and pharmaceutical industries.[18] They suggested that these patterns resulted from factors related to the high levels of market concentration in those industries. Several studies of antitrust violations have produced empirical support, albeit modest, for the contention that high market concentration is positively correlated with corporate crime.[19]

Despite the fact that these empirical findings were produced in quantitative cross-sectional and longitudinal studies, a general theoretical framework for understanding their significance emerged largely out of case studies of white-collar crime in particular industries. In a study of the automobile industry, William Leonard and Marvin Weber focused on the "criminogenic market forces" within the industry—particularly the high levels of market concentration—that induced and facilitated criminal behavior.[20] Likewise, Harvey Farberman stressed that the oligopolistic nature of the automobile industry enabled the manufacturers to create a market structure that virtually required lower-level industry participants to engage in illegal activity.[21] Norman Denzin developed similar themes in his analysis of the American liquor industry, in which he found that the multitiered structure of the industry was linked to both "crimes of competition," such as bribery and kickbacks, and "crimes of cooperation," such as price-fixing.[22]

Martin and Carolyn Needleman added a theoretical refinement to this discussion by observing that the studies described above focused on what they called "crime-coercive systems"—systems in which organizations coerce their employees into illegal behavior for the benefit of the organization. Other industries, they argued, are better characterized as "crime-facilitative systems" in which "criminal activity [is] an unwelcome but unavoidable cost of doing business."[23] In crime-facilitative systems, the industry as a whole does not benefit from the crime, but illegal activity is a by-product of certain arrangements that allow industry members to achieve their legitimate goals. As an example, Needleman and Needleman point to the securities industry where secrecy laws that help to cloak frauds are also beneficial to legitimate investment banks. This notion is very useful in understanding how it is that the legitimate members of criminogenic industries tolerate fraud and abuse in their midst.

Economists George Ackerlof and Paul Romer followed a similar line of reasoning in their account of "looting" in financial institutions. They posited that government guarantees on private sector debt—as in the U.S. savings and loan industry in the 1980s—inevitably creates "perverse incentives" for firms to engage in "bankruptcy for profit." Applying their theory to a diverse set of financial crises, they argued that "bankruptcy-for-profit will occur if poor accounting, lax regulation, or low penalties for abuse give owners an incentive to pay themselves more than their firms are worth and then default on their debt obligations."[24]

In all of these theoretical accounts, economic actors are

responding rationally, if not ethically, to market inducements to engage in illegal activity. As Mark Granovetter has pointed out, the "self-interest" of actors in the marketplace may be just as easily pursued by malfeasance and fraud as by legitimate means.[25]

Legislation and regulatory policies also have an important role in creating these market inducements. In their formulation of a "strain" theory of organizational crime, Henry Finney and Henry Lesieur observed that: "[a] common source of environmental strain is the law itself" and that "changes in laws are often a primary cause of criminal behavior by organizations . . . [as] the new laws impose new operating cost constraints and are therefore a major external source of strain."[26] Andrew Szasz described an illustration of this process in his examination of the illegal toxic waste disposal industry. There he showed how the enactment of stricter federal regulatory standards covering the disposal of hazardous industrial waste created incentives for legitimate businesses to contract with waste haulers that had organized crime connections to illegally dump their toxic waste. In effect, this situation allowed legitimate businesses to "externalize criminogenesis."[27]

While new regulatory laws may create incentives for crime, *deregulatory* legislation may also produce widespread criminality. The best example of this is found in the savings and loan industry where "the deregulation of the 1980s [transformed] the industry virtually overnight, precipitating its demise, and opening up opportunities both to those seeking windfall profits from high-risk investments and to those who used the industry as their personal 'money machine.'"[28]

Moreover, regulatory laws can combine with industry conditions to produce *criminogenic market segments*. While an industry as a whole may not be criminogenic or is relatively noncriminogenic, certain segments of the industry may be highly vulnerable to fraud and abuse. This occurs when dominant firms in an industry abandon segments of that industry because they lack profitability or represent excessive risk. This exodus leaves the door open to fraudulent operators who take advantage of the firms' departure to defraud stranded consumers. A good illustration of this process is found in inner-city neighborhoods where banks, following a practice known as *redlining,* essentially stop making residential mortgage loans, and the market is taken over by unscrupulous mortgage companies who charge residents usurious rates on home loans. In Boston, for example, large banks profited from such a situation by buying the loans from the mortgage companies and earning interest at rates far above what they would normally charge, while someone else enforced the loan agreements.[29] This example illustrates the point that, consistent with the concept of crime-facilitative systems, business leaders in the larger industry may tolerate criminal misconduct in the criminogenic market segment, and even resist change to the system, because the same conditions that give rise to crime and abuse there may greatly benefit them.

This is the situation that exists in the small business health insurance industry. As in other markets for illegal goods and services, such as illicit drugs, criminal enterprises in the small group health insurance industry exist because of unmet consumer demand. Over the past several decades, the departure of legitimate insurance companies from the small group market has resulted in millions of Americans being unable to obtain affordable health care coverage. Many have been forced to turn to con artists, who have taken advantages of loopholes in regulatory laws to market health insurance without the normal safeguards that surround the legitimate insurance industry.

Thus, the small business health insurance industry possesses the features of a criminogenic industry. This is not to say that all providers of insurance in the market are corrupt. Indeed, the vast majority of these plans are legitimate and their operators honest. Rather, it is to say that the structure of the industry and its regulatory environment create vast opportunities for fraud that result in a continuous flow of unscrupulous con artists into the market. As in the illicit drug market, because the demand is so high and the potential for profit so great, even when law enforcement agents successfully shut down a fraudulent health insurance scheme, others quickly pop up to take its place. Exactly how this happens is described in detail in later chapters.

DATA AND METHODS

This book is based on a study that began with a focus on three states—California, Florida, and Texas—where small business health insurance fraud had been particularly common and its consequences most severe.[30] However, it soon became clear that these criminal schemes operate nationwide and that while many of their victims may have been located in these three states, the individuals behind the schemes may have been elsewhere. Thus, the scope of the study was expanded to more of a national perspective.

The study relied on a variety of different data sources. The case studies, which comprise the bulk of the book, were assembled from a diverse set of sources that include government reports, newspaper articles, articles in trade periodicals, congressional hearings, and internal agency reports. Probably the most important source, however, consisted of documents found in court cases—both civil and criminal—involving those accused of participating in illegal insurance schemes. These documents, while tedious to review and assemble, provided a rich source of descriptive information about the mechanics of these fraudulent schemes. These materials represent an underutilized source of data for white-collar crime researchers and, with the advent of electronic databases, an increasingly accessible source.

In addition to these data sources, interviews were conducted with prosecutors, federal law enforcement agents, investigators at state regulatory agencies, and policy analysts.[31] Two of these individuals were interviewed via telephone, but the rest were interviewed face to face. Approximately half of the interviews were taped and transcribed. Where taping was deemed intrusive, handwritten notes of the interviews were kept. Interviews lasted from as little as 20 minutes to as long as 3½ hours.

Follow-up discussions were held with several of those individuals interviewed, either face to face or via telephone. In these follow-ups, more specific information about individuals or cases was often elicited that helped in the interpretation of court documents and in making connections between individuals, events, and organizations.

White-collar crime researchers traditionally have relied on the case study approach to address their subject. The reasons for this are several. First, as Edwin Sutherland (who coined the term *white-collar crime*) argued in the 1940s, there is very little official data on white-collar crime, a particularly striking fact when one considers the abundance of data on street-level crime.[32] Second, because of the secretive nature of these criminal events—the fact that many of them take place behind corporate doors—and the ability of their perpetrators to evade questioning by social scientists, methods such as surveys are difficult to employ.[33] As a result, case studies of individual instances of white-collar crime that draw on multiple sources of data have been the norm in much white-collar crime research.

Yet the case study is not simply a default strategy, a less productive approach used simply because more rigorous methods are not possible. Rather, the case study has its own advantages over more quantitative approaches. As Anthony Orum, Joe Feagin, and Gideon Sjoberg have written: "(1) [The case study] permits the grounding of observations and concepts about social action and social structures in natural settings studied at close hand. (2) It provides information from a number of sources and over a period of time. . . . (3) It can furnish the dimensions of time and history to the study of social life."[34]

The most problematic aspect of this method is a question of sampling: How do we know that the cases we chose are representative of the larger population of events about which we wish to speak? John Walton provides a succinct answer: "Case studies get at the causal texture of social life, but drift without anchor unless they are incorporated into some typology of general processes, made causally explicit within the case, and ultimately referred back to the universe which the case represents."[35] In other words, in choosing cases the researcher first has to construct a "typology of general processes"—a set of relevant characteristics—and then make sure that the cases studied embody or exemplify these characteristics. In selecting the cases described herein, Walton's recommendation was followed. The cases chosen represent the different forms that small business health insurance fraud takes and illustrate their fundamental characteristics.

In the process of putting together case studies the investigator often functions less as an academic researcher and more as a detective. Connections must be made between individuals, motives must be attributed, and chronologies of events must be established. As William Sanders has observed:

[B]oth sociologists and detectives formulate theories and develop methods in an attempt to answer two general questions: "Why did it happen," and "In what circumstances is it likely to happen again?"—that is, to explain and predict.[36]

Yet, in contrast to the detective, for the sociological researcher the goal is not to produce an iron-clad case that will provide the basis for a successful prosecution, but instead to learn enough about each case so that it can be fitted into the general analysis. As Walton suggests, the substance of the case must always relate back to the general argument being made and the broader issues being considered, by way of illustration or example. At the same time, variations in cases help to demonstrate the diversity of the phenomenon under study and, ultimately, people's ingenuity and creativity in improvising new strategies to meet changing conditions, so that it is important not to seek too rigid a correspondence between case materials and theoretical arguments.

OVERVIEW OF THE BOOK

The book is organized as follows. Chapter 1 describes the structural sources of the problem that were briefly summarized here in the Introduction. Changes in the small group health insurance market and in the regulatory environment are shown to have created both the demand for illegal health insurance and the means by which white-collar criminals could provide it. The chapter also briefly describes the three principal forms that insider health insurance fraud has taken.

The next four chapters provide detailed case studies that demonstrate how these schemes are carried out. Chapter 2 describes frauds involving multiple employer welfare arrangements (MEWAS). It shows how a good idea, one that seeks to create alternative mechanisms for providing health insurance, can go terribly wrong. Chapter 3 looks at cases involving what are known as employee leasing firms, which offer what appears to be legitimate health insurance to the employees of small business but which turn out to be simply Ponzi schemes. Chapter 4 examines health insurance scams involving bogus labor unions. This chapter focuses on a series of related cases that began with two individuals on Long Island, New York, and evolved into an extraordinarily complex network of insurance crooks who bilked thousands of individuals out of millions of dollars in insurance premiums. Chapter 4 introduces the concept of *recombinant fraud,* a form of white-collar crime that continually evolves to meet changing conditions. Chapter 5 takes a close look at several innovations in insurance fraud among companies claiming not to be in the business of selling insurance. It begins with two new cases involving bogus labor union schemes. The chapter then presents yet another twist on insurance swindles: organizations that evade regulation by claiming to be religious, mutual help groups rather than insurance providers. Not all of these programs are fraudulent; many are well intentioned but place their participants at risk nonetheless. All of them raise fundamental questions about the definition of insurance and the role of the state in protecting consumers.

Chapter 6 returns to questions of policy. If the roots of the problem lie in an ambiguous set of laws, at least in part, then the solution seems clear: Change the laws. Yet this has not happened. The reasons for this inaction—the political economy that surrounds legislative debate on this issue—are discussed in this chapter.

In the final chapter, findings from the preceding chapters are summarized, conclusions are drawn, and broader implications are discussed. There we shall see that health insurance frauds of the type examined here raise basic questions about the nature of white-collar crime and its traditional separation from both violent crime and organized crime. The concept of recombinant fraud is discussed in more detail and linked to changing patterns in the labor market and in the organization of business in the global economy. Finally, broader issues of policy are discussed, with a focus on the limits of a marketplace that operates free of government oversight to provide such a basic service as health insurance in a society where health care is increasingly a precious and much fought-over commodity.

NOTES

1 *In re* Consolidated Welfare Fund ERISA Litigation, *Bailey v. Empire Blue Cross,* 856 F. Supp. 837.

2 Senate Committee on Governmental Affairs, Permanent Subcommittee on Investigations, *Fraud and Abuse in Employer Sponsored Health Benefit Plans,* statement of Jo Ann Howard, Texas State Board of Insurance, 101st Cong., 2d sess., 15 May 1990, 112.

3 House Committee on Energy and Commerce, Subcommittee on Oversight and Investigations, *Failed Promises: Insurance Company Insolvencies,* 101st Cong., 2d sess., February 1990, 1.

4 Diane Vaughan has observed that some organizations may be particularly susceptible to fraud because of the "nature of transactions" within

the organization. The form that transactions take create opportunities for fraud by: "(1) providing legitimate mechanisms that can be used to pursue scarce resources unlawfully and (2) further minimizing risk of detection and sanctioning." Diane Vaughan, *Controlling Unlawful Organizational Behavior* (Chicago: University of Chicago Press, 1983), 76.

5 In 1992, the GAO estimated that 10 percent of all health care costs go to fraud and abuse. General Accounting Office, *Health Insurance: Vulnerable Payers Lose Billions to Fraud and Abuse*, GAO/T–HRD–92–29, 1992, p. 2. The most recent data for health care expenditures are for 1994 and show total health care expenditures totaling $949 billion. Assuming that 1994–1995 growth rates will be similar to the 1993–1994 rate of change (6.4 percent), as some analysts do, one can estimate that expenditures for 1995 exceeded $1 trillion. Katherine Levit, Helen Lazenby, and Lakha Sivaraja, "Health Care Spending in 1994: Slowest in Decades," *Health Affairs* 15 (1996): 130–44.

6 The $175 billion represents an estimate of the direct costs associated with paying off depositors at failed savings and loans. The long-term costs, including the interest paid by the government on bonds sold to finance the bailout, could be as high as $500 billion. Kitty Calavita, Henry Pontell, and Robert Tillman, *Big Money Crime: Fraud and Politics in the Savings and Loan Crisis* (Berkeley: University of California Press, 1997), 1.

7 General Accounting Office, *Employee Benefits: States Need Labor's Help Regulating Multiple Employer Welfare Arrangements*, GAO/HRD–92–40, March 1992, p. 2.

8 Employment Benefit Research Institute, *Sources of Health Insurance and Characteristics of the Uninsured* (Washington, D.C.: Employment Benefit Research Institute, 1996).

9 See, for example, David Himmelstein and Steffie Woolhandler, "Care Denied: U.S. Residents Who Are Unable to Obtain Needed Medical Services," *American Journal of Public Health* 3 (1995): 341–44.

10 Suzy Hagstrom, "Broken Promises: Clients Left Unsupported by Insurance Groups," *Orlando Sentinel Tribune*, 25 June 1990, p. 1.

11 Joseph Gusfield, *The Culture of Public Problems: Drinking-Driving and the Symbolic Order* (Chicago: University of Chicago Press, 1981).

12 National Coalition Against Insurance Fraud, "Discussion Paper: Fraud Bureau Funding" (n.d.).

13 Robert Ceniceros and Joanne Wojcik, "California Fraud Cops, Regulators Trade Charges," *Business Insurance*, 12 August 1996, p. 1.

14 National Insurance Crime Bureau, "Insurance Fraud: The $20 Billion Disaster" (n.d.).

15 Senate Special Committee on Aging, *Gaming the Health Care System: Trends in Health Care Fraud*, testimony of Louis Freeh, Director of

the Federal Bureau of Investigation, 104th Cong., 1st sess., 21 March 1995, 43.

16 *Green v. NAPE,* No. 92-CV-424 (S.D.N.Y. 1992).

17 Edwin Sutherland, *White-Collar Crime: The Uncut Version* (New Haven: Yale University Press, [1949] 1983), 19.

18 Marshall Clinard and Peter Yeager, *Corporate Crime* (Glencoe, Ill.: Free Press, 1980), 119.

19 Peter Asch and Joseph Seneca, "Characteristics of Collusive Firms," *Journal of Industrial Economics* 23 (1975): 223–47; Sally Simpson, "The Decomposition of Antitrust: Testing a Multi-level, Longitudinal Model of Profit-Squeeze," *American Sociological Review* 51 (1986): 859–75.

20 William Leonard and Marvin Weber, "Automakers and Dealers: A Study of Criminogenic Market Forces," *Law and Society Review* 4 (1970): 407–24.

21 Harvey Farberman, "A Criminogenic Market Structure: The Automobile Industry," *Sociological Quarterly* 16 (1975): 456.

22 Norman Denzin, "Notes on the Criminogenic Hypothesis: A Case Study of the American Liquor Industry," *American Sociological Review* 42 (1977): 919.

23 Martin Needleman and Carolyn Needleman, "Organizational Crime: Two Models of Criminogenesis," *Sociological Quarterly* 20 (1979): 521.

24 George Ackerlof and Paul Romer, "Looting: the Economic Underworld of Bankruptcy for Profit," Department of Economics, University of California, Berkeley, 1993, p. 1.

25 Mark Granovetter, "Economic Action and Social Structure: The Problem of Embeddedness," in *The Sociology of Economic Life,* ed. Mark Granovetter and Richard Swedberg (Boulder, Col.: West View Press, 1992), 58–63.

26 Henry Finney and Henry Lesieur, "A Contingency Theory of Organizational Crime," in *Research in the Sociology of Organizations,* vol. 1, ed. Samuel Bacharach (Greenwich: JAI Press, 1982), 273.

27 Andrew Szasz, "Corporations, Organized Crime, and the Disposal of Hazardous Waste," *Criminology* 24 (1986): 22.

28 Kitty Calavita and Henry Pontell, "The Savings and Loan Industry," in *Above the Law: Crime in Complex Organizations,* ed. Michael Tonry and Albert Reiss (Chicago: University of Chicago Press, 1993), 212.

29 Peter Conellos and Steve Marantz, "AG to Probe Possible Ties of Banks to Unfair Loans," *Boston Globe,* 7 May 1991, p. 1; Peter Conellos and Gary Chafetz, "Mortgage Companies Got Credit from Fleet," *Boston Globe,* 8 May 1991, p. 1.

30 Robert Tillman, "Controlling Fraud in the Small Business Health Insurance Industry," final report to the National Institute of Justice, 1998.

31 For a fuller discussion of the methods employed, see Tillman, ibid.

32 Edwin Sutherland, *White-Collar Crime: The Uncut Version,* (New Haven: Yale University Press, [1949] 1983).

33 Gilbert Geis, "The Case Study Method in Sociological Criminology," in *A Case for the Case Study,* ed. Anthony Orum, Joe Feagin, and Gideon Sjoberg (Chapel Hill: University of North Carolina Press, 1991), 208.

34 Anthony Orum, Joe Feagin and Gideon Sjoberg, "The Nature of the Case Study," in *A Case for the Case Study* (Chapel Hill: University of North Carolina Press, 1991), 6–7.

35 John Walton, "Making the Theoretical Case," in *What is a Case? Exploring the Foundations of Social Inquiry,* ed. Charles Ragin and Howard Becker (Cambridge: Cambridge University Press, 1992), 124.

36 William B. Sanders, "The Methods and Evidence of Detectives and Sociologists," in *The Sociologist as Detective: An Introduction to Research Methods,* 2d ed., ed. William B. Sanders (New York: Praeger, 1976), 1.

The Health Care Crisis and Health Insurance Fraud

IN early 1994, as President Clinton was proposing his ill-fated health care reform package, reports were appearing almost daily in the media declaring a "health care crisis" in America.[1] The chief culprit was costs. Throughout the 1980s and into the 1990s, annual increases in health care expenditures outpaced inflation by significant margins.[2] As a result, many Americans simply could no longer afford health insurance. Hardest hit were small business owners and their employees, who saw their health insurance premiums go through the roof and often times their policies disappear altogether.

One member of this group was Karen Allen, a 47-year-old employee of a floor-covering business in Kensington, Maryland. In November 1987, Allen, her 24-year-old daughter, and a coworker enrolled in a health insurance program sponsored by Blue Cross Blue Shield. Their combined premiums totaled $324 a month. One year later, despite the fact that none of the three had submitted a major claim, Blue Cross raised their combined monthly premiums to $400—an increase of 23 percent—and cut back their benefits. A year later Blue Cross informed the group that their rates were increasing again to $743 per month, representing an increase of 130 percent in just two years. Allen's premiums alone had gone up to $379 a month, amounting to 50 percent of her take-home pay![3]

Allen, her daughter, and coworker were among millions of Americans who in the late 1980s were abandoned by the health insurance industry and thus the health care system. They were victims of massive changes that transformed the private health insurance industry in the 1970s and 1980s. One of these changes was the departure of most major insurers from the small group market for the simple reason that it was no longer profitable. Many small business employees and self-employed individuals found themselves victimized twice: first, when insurance companies refused to write them affordable health care policies, and second, when they were ripped off by insurance scam artists who sold them policies at below-market costs, claiming that an obscure law known as ERISA gave them a financial advantage over health insurance companies.

Thus, to understand how these crooks have been able, with seeming impunity, to steal millions of dollars from people who desperately needed medical coverage, we must look at both the changes in the health insurance industry and the regulatory changes brought about by the Employee Retirement Income Security Act (ERISA).

THE HEALTH INSURANCE INDUSTRY

In the past several decades, three major changes have transformed the health insurance industry: (1) the increasing tendency for large firms to self-insure, (2) the emergence of managed care networks, and (3) the utilization of extremely restrictive underwriting practices by insurers in the small group market.

Self-Insurance

Ironically, the departure of major insurance companies from the health insurance market was a response, in large part, to a drop in demand for their products, not by small businesses but by large corporations. Since the early decades of the twentieth century, large companies provided health care benefits to their employees by purchasing group policies from insurance companies. This pattern began to change dramatically in 1974 when Congress enacted ERISA. One of ERISA's impacts was to change the health insurance regulatory landscape forever.

Historically, regulation of the insurance industry in the United States has been left to the states rather than to the federal government.[4] Insurance companies must be licensed by the states in which they operate and must conform with state requirements, including the maintenance of minimum capital reserves, the payment of premium taxes, and the provision of certain "mandated benefits" (that is, coverage of specific illnesses and health conditions, all of which add dollars to the premiums paid by employers and employees). ERISA provided employers with a mechanism for significantly reducing these costs by giving them the option to *self-insure*, that is, to bypass the insurance companies altogether and create their own self-funded insurance plans. Significantly, self-insured plans were deemed *employee welfare benefit plans* as defined by ERISA and were therefore exempt from state regulation. By self-insuring, companies not only avoided paying for the insurance companies' profit margins but also the costs associated with state requirements.

Large corporations, faced with mounting health benefit costs, quickly saw the advantages of self-insurance and rapidly began dropping their group plans and setting up their own plans. By 1987, approximately 65 percent of all companies with 1,000 or more employees were self-insured.[5]

Unlike large firms, small businesses find it difficult to self-insure because of simple cost factors related to their size. First, it is difficult to apply actuarial principles to assess risk among groups whose numbers are small. Second, administrative costs for small group plans are much higher than they are for large firms, thus raising the premiums for individual employees. For example, one study found that administrative expenses for firms with 1 to 4 employees averaged 40 percent of claims, while for large firms with 10,000 or more employees the average was 5.5 percent.[6] This puts small businesses at a real disadvantage when competing with large companies for employee health insurance.

The Growth of Managed Care Networks

The other development that has altered the health insurance market in recent years has been the dramatic growth in *managed care networks,* the two principal forms of which are *health maintenance organizations* (HMOs) and *preferred provider organizations* (PPOs).[7] Between 1980 and 1987, enrollment in HMOs increased from 9 million to 32 million.[8] By 1994, that number had increased to 42 million.[9] In only three years, 1984 to 1987, enrollment in PPOs skyrocketed from 1.3 million to 17.5 million.[10]

This trend reflected the decision by many employers to switch from private insurance plans to the generally less expensive managed care plans. However, at the same time, in order to reduce their costs, employers have increased the average contributions from employees and, in some cases, discouraged individual employees from extending their coverage to their families.[11]

These trends have drastically reduced the market for traditional commercial health insurance, and insurers who remain in the market have been forced to engage in more aggressive underwriting practices.[12]

Cherry Picking:
The Shift to Restrictive Underwriting Practices

Historically, commercial insurers grouped individuals into larger "communities" determined by geographical location or by employer type. Insurers set premiums based on these community-rated plans, and all subscribers paid the same premium. The theory underlying this practice was that "low-cost" individuals—younger, healthier persons—would evenly share the cost of health care with "high-cost" individuals—older, less healthy persons. Under this system, low-cost individuals tend to subsidize the health needs of high-cost individuals.

Beginning in the 1940s, a number of commercial insurers began to challenge the dominance of the major health insurance companies (as well as Blue Cross Blue Shield plans) by undercutting their rates with *experience-rated* plans. Under experience rating, "the past experience of the group to be insured is used to determine the premium."[13] Groups that consist of younger, healthier employees, for example, receive lower rates than groups that consist of generally older, less healthy employees. Occupations involving more hazardous work pay higher premiums than groups involved in less hazardous jobs. By shifting to experience-rated plans, insurance companies could offer cheaper rates to generally healthy groups.

Inevitably, the competitive advantage enjoyed by insurers who offered experience-rated health plans changed the entire market. Today, almost all commercial health insurers as well as the Blues offer plans based on some form of experience rating.

By the 1980s, with most larger companies choosing to self-insure and many other employers turning to HMOs, most of the major insurers simply left the health insurance market; those that still offered health insurance plans tended to exclude small groups and individuals.[14] Insurers who remained in the small business market realized that to turn a profit they would have to take experience rating to its extreme by engaging in extremely restrictive underwriting practices that ensured that only the low-cost healthy employees would enroll in their plans. In other words, to maximize profits, insurers began to take only the most "desirable" participants, in terms of potential costs to insurers, leaving the "undesirables" to fend for themselves. To guarantee a healthy group of policyholders, insurers began employing several specific policies: (1) redlining certain occupations, (2) denying coverage to persons with a wide range of preexisting conditions, and (3) writing policies on a short-term, nonguarantee basis.

/ REDLINING / Just as commercial banks deny loans to residents of certain neighborhoods because of their perceived higher likelihood of default, so do insurance companies deny health coverage to individuals in occupations deemed hazardous or to individuals thought to "overutilize" health care. Insurance companies are understandably reluctant to speak publicly about these practices, but a number of investigations have revealed that redlining is a widespread practice in the insurance industry. One study found that seven out of the nation's ten largest insurers in the small business health insurance market routinely engage in this form of redlining occupations.[15]

A 1990 analysis by the General Accounting Office (GAO) discovered that large numbers of insurers refused to write policies not only for individuals in occupations with high probabilities of accidents and injuries, such as logging and mining, but also in a wide range of other occupations. Included were (1) physicians and lawyers, "because [insurance companies] believe it is too difficult to deal with fraud, abuse and litigation for small firms in these areas"; (2) "entertainment and sports industries because of the high risk of drug abuse treatment costs"; and (3) "barbers, beauticians and decorators because of concerns with the higher costs of AIDS and sexually transmitted diseases."[16] Many insurers also refuse to write group policies for employees of restaurants, bars, and other establishments that sell alcoholic beverages because employees of these establishments are believed to have a greater tendency towards alcoholism.[17] Some of these individuals are able to afford expensive individual policies from Blue Cross/Blue Shield, but many more simply remain uninsured.

/ PREEXISTING CONDITIONS / Even if an individual is not in a high-risk occupation, he or she may find it nearly impossible to find health insurance coverage because they have or may potentially have a health condition that requires expensive medical treatment. In the parlance of the insurance industry, these are known as *preexisting conditions,* and they effectively eliminate large portions of the population from eligibility for health insurance. Individuals may be denied coverage because of a history of serious problems such as heart attacks or cancer, and entire groups of employees, if their combined numbers are small, may be disqualified because of the medical history of a single individual. In these latter cases, the insurer may either deny insurance to the whole group, increase premiums by imposing a high surcharge, or refuse to write policies for the individuals with preexisting conditions.[18] The increasingly common use of these tactics creates a Catch-22 situation in which the people who need health insurance the most, those with ongoing health problems, are the least likely to obtain it.[19]

/ NO GUARANTEE OF RENEWAL / Finally, just because a group of employees has obtained health insurance coverage does not mean they are guaranteed coverage in the future. A growing trend among health insurers is to offer coverage to employees of small businesses on a *nonguarantee issue* basis. Policies are written for a limited period, often six months to one year, and no guarantee is made that the same contract will be offered at the same rate in following years. After the initial contract expires the insurer may cancel the entire group policy, exclude certain employees from participation, or dramatically increase premiums.[20] Thus, a single pregnancy or illness among a group of small business employees may cause the group's overall rates to increase from 40 to 60 percent.[21]

Taken together, these practices are part of a broad strategy known as *cherry picking* in which insurers attempt to maximize profits by covering the healthiest, least costly members of the small group market and ignoring the rest. These predatory practices have spread throughout the small business market, and even reputable insurers have been forced to comply with the new rules of the game. As one health insurance analyst put it, "If an insurance company allows its competitors to skim off workers and firms who are good risks, it will be left with 'demographic sludge' and a greater probability of losing money or being priced out of the market."[22]

One of the best examples of cherry picking is found in the underwriting policies of a company called Golden Rule Insurance Company. In 1994, Golden Rule was the largest writer of individual health policies in the country. According to one critic, "this company's business mantra is to attract usually young, unwitting consumers with policies that have low front-end costs, but which over time become either very expensive or very limited in what coverage they actually provide."[23] One of the keys to Golden Rule's financial success was its policy of selective underwriting; coverage was denied to anyone who appeared to have any potential for serious health problems. Prospective policyholders were asked to detail their medical histories over the last ten years, including descriptions of such common conditions as pregnancy, back pain, asthma, and sinus problems. Applicants were also required to supply the names of every physician they had seen in the last five years and to give the company permission to obtain medical information from those physicians. Golden Rule's policies specified a large number of conditions that were excluded from coverage.

One policyholder who learned the hard way about Golden Rule's aggressive underwriting practices was Kelly Wert. In 1993, Wert was a 22-year-old Virginian and recent college graduate with aspirations of becoming a high school English teacher. When she graduated from college, she learned that her family's health plan, provided by the Travelers Insurance Company, would no longer cover her as a dependent. After seeing a flyer on campus, she purchased a three-month policy from Golden Rule, which she later extended for another three months. It was during the latter term that Wert learned that a rare medical disorder she had been afflicted with for a number of years—a nervous disorder that caused her arm to jerk up and down uncontrollably—had gotten worse and would require expensive surgery to correct. Her parents had contacted surgical experts in New York who had agreed to perform the complicated surgery, which involved drilling into her skull and destroying the brain cells that were causing the disorder. At this point Golden Rule informed Wert that they would not pay for the $44,000 surgery because they regarded it as a pre-existing condition. After her plight was detailed in the newspaper in her hometown of Roanoke, Virginia, neighbors and family friends held benefits to raise money to help pay for the surgery. Then in mid-February 1994, the Wert family learned that Travelers had decided to pay for the surgery under the parents' original policy. The next month, Wert's surgery was successfully performed.[24]

Another Roanoke resident and Golden Rule policyholder, Daniel Brokaw, was not so lucky. In 1992, Brokaw, a 42-year-old self-employed electrician, purchased a policy from Golden Rule. His policy excluded from coverage any treatments related to Brokaw's case of Tourette's syndrome, an ailment that causes nervous tics, which he controlled with medication. Furthermore, Golden Rule refused to provide any health benefits to Brokaw's 4-year-old son because the boy occasionally shook his fist in what they saw as possible early evidence of Tourette's syndrome but that the boy's doctor said could simply be a common childhood gesture.[25]

Golden Rule's defenders argued that they were simply using good business principles by denying coverage to those with preexisting conditions. The company's president, John Whelan, defended the practice by arguing that selling insurance to an individual who "has already suffered the condition for which the coverage is sought may be charitable, but it is not the business of insurance. Fire insurance is not provided after the house catches fire."[26]

More than simply engaging in aggressive underwriting, Golden Rule's executives fought hard in a number of states to defeat legislation that would have made health insurance more accessible by prohibiting many of the practices that had brought the company handsome profits over the years.[27] In 1992, when Colorado legislators were considering a bill that would have prohibited some of the more egregious forms of cherry picking by insurers, Golden Rule hired a telemarketing firm to call small business owners in the state to urge them to tell their representatives to vote against the bill.[28] In its home state of Indiana, the company tried a more direct approach. A company lobbyist left envelopes with checks for $100 to $250 on the desks of state legislators inside the House chambers.[29] After Vermont legislators proposed bills that would have required insurers to offer policies based on community ratings rather than experience ratings, Golden Rule's president held a press conference on the steps of the statehouse. With him were two ferrets in cages with labels that read "the Gov" (the state's governor) and "the Commish" (the state insurance commissioner).[30]

Golden Rule later became the subject of considerable media attention when it was revealed that the firm had aggressively lobbied Republican members of Congress to push for legislation that would have given tax breaks to individuals who set up *medical savings accounts* (MSAs). Medical savings accounts allow individuals to establish tax-free trusts to pay for their future health care costs. As a leader among firms offering MSAs, Golden Rule would have profited handsomely if the legislation had passed. According to official records, Golden Rule contributed $620,775 to Republicans in the 1993–1994 campaign cycle.[31]

As a result of practices such as those employed by Golden Rule, many small businesses cannot access or afford health insurance for their employees, a problem that is reflected in statistics on the uninsured. The proportion of nonelderly uninsured in the population increased from 14.6 percent in 1979 to 17.5 percent in 1986, and by 1995 was 17.4 percent of the population, representing 40.3 million individuals.[32] The problem is not simply one of poverty and unemployment. In 1995, nearly 80 percent of the nonelderly uninsured lived in households whose head was employed at least part time.[33] Surveys have shown that the likelihood that a worker is insured is highly influenced by the size of his or her employer. In 1987,

51 percent of uninsured workers were employed by companies with 25 or fewer employees. In 1988, only 40 percent of those firms with less than 10 workers offered their employees health plans.[34] Studies have shown that the primary reason why small employers do not offer health plans to their employees is cost—they simply cannot afford it.[35]

Thus, the problem appears to be one of supply, not demand. This is not to say that even if offered access to health care insurance, all employees would enroll. Rather, it is to assert that there exists a substantial number of workers in this country who would like to have health insurance for themselves and their dependents but are unable to because of cost or availability.

In this environment, where demand for health benefits among small business employees is high and supply in the legitimate market is low, crooks have been able to thrive by creating what constitutes a black market in health insurance.

THE REGULATORY ENVIRONMENT

While unmet demand for health insurance created the opportunities for white-collar crime, it was changes in the law, specifically ERISA, that created the means to commit these crimes. By recognizing the legal status of entities that could sell insurance outside of any meaningful regulation, Congress created the "organizational weapons" that white-collar criminals would use to defraud millions of Americans.[36]

ERISA

Following the failure of several large pension funds in the late 1960s and early 1970s, concern grew about the unregulated character of these funds and the potential for fraud and mismanagement among those who administered them.[37] In response, in 1974 Congress passed the landmark Employee Retirement Income Security Act (ERISA), which imposed federal regulations on private pension funds by creating standards for eligibility, vesting, and financing and by requiring contributions to a guaranty insurance fund for pension plans. Provisions of the act extended beyond pensions and into employee benefits generally, including employer-sponsored health insurance plans.[38]

One of the purposes of the law was to allow "employee welfare benefit plans" to market health insurance to employees. The law defined "employee welfare benefit plans" as "any plan, fund, or program . . . established or maintained by an employer or by an employee organization . . . maintained for the purpose of providing for its participants or beneficiaries, through the purchase of insurance or otherwise, . . . medical, surgical, or hospital care or benefits, or benefits in the event of sickness, accident, disability, death."[39] ERISA recognized two fundamental types of employee benefit plans: (1) single employer self-insurance plans, and (2) multiple employer welfare benefit plans, sometimes referred to as *multiple employer trusts* (METS). The idea behind the creation of these multiple employer plans was to give employees of small businesses access to the same affordable health insurance as the employees of large firms by allowing employers to pool their employees for insurance purposes. Pooling arrangements bring down rates by creating a mix of high-risk and low-risk participants whose costs balance one another out and by creating an economy of scale that reduces administrative expenses.

One important provision of ERISA known as the *deemer clause* stated that "neither an employee benefit plan, nor any trust established under such a plan shall be deemed to be engaged in the business of insurance for the purpose of any state insurance laws."[40] Thus, state insurance commissions did not maintain regulatory authority over employee benefit plans. Operators of multiple employer welfare benefit plans could claim exemption from state oversight because the federal law "preempted" state regulation. While ERISA imposed rigorous standards on pension plans, it imposed virtually none of the standards common to state-regulated insurance plans—minimum funding standards, mandated benefits, or contributions to a guaranty fund—on employee benefit plans. Moreover, while ERISA required these METs to be registered with the U.S. Department of Labor, it did not require their owners to actually obtain any form of certification before marketing their plans.[41]

Thus, one of the unintended consequences of ERISA was to create a regulatory vacuum in which employee benefit plans, in their various forms, could operate without the oversight extended to licensed insurance companies. As a result, soon after ERISA was enacted white-collar criminals began using its ambiguities and loopholes to perpetrate frauds against unsuspecting employers and employees. Many of these schemes involved METs that were simply Ponzi schemes: their operators were able to collect premiums from policyholders without paying off on claims for long periods of time while keeping regulators at bay by claiming an ERISA preemption from state regulation.[42]

Among the early MET scams was an organization known as National Health Care Trust, based in Chicago. The company's operators took in millions of dollars in premiums from the employees of 82 nursing homes in Illinois and diverted nearly half of the total for administrative expenses and commissions. When state regulators shut the company down in 1982, it left nearly $400,000 in unpaid claims. When first confronted by regulators, the company's owners claimed ERISA exemption from state regulation; during the subsequent year-long effort by state officials to verify their claim, the owners continued to take in premiums from unwitting victims.[43] As a harbinger of a pattern that would become all too familiar in later years, the operators of National Health Care Trust created that organization soon after an earlier plan they ran was shut down by regulators, leaving hundreds of employees with thousands of dollars in unpaid medical bills.[44]

MEWA Fraud

These abuses came to public light in 1982 congressional hearings chaired by Rep. John Erlenborn.[45] The next year Congress enacted new legislation that attempted to eliminate the ERISA loopholes. The new law, known as the Erlenborn amendments, defined a new employee benefit plan—multiple employer welfare arrangements (MEWAS)—and attempted to clarify regulatory jurisdiction over these and related entities.[46] MEWAS were defined as:

an employee welfare benefit plan, or any other arrangement (other than an employer welfare benefit plan), which is established or maintained for the purpose of offering or providing any benefit . . . to the employees of two or more employers (including one or more self-employed individuals), or to their beneficiaries, except that such term does not include any such plan or other arrangement which is established or maintained—(i) under or pursuant to one or more agreements which the Secretary finds to be collective bargaining agreements, or (ii) by a rural electric cooperative.[47]

MEWAS, like METS, can take three forms: fully insured, partially insured, and self-funded. Under fully insured arrangements, a licensed insurance company provides full coverage to the association and handles the administration of the plan. Under partially insured arrangements, insurance companies provide the coverage but a third-party administrator is responsible for administering the plan. Self-funded MEWAS, as their name implies, provide all coverage themselves and may be administered by a third party.[48] Under the amended version of ERISA, fully insured MEWAS were to be exempt from state regulation except for state laws regarding "the maintenance of specified levels of reserves and specified levels of contributions."[49] MEWA plans that are not fully insured—for example, self-funded plans—are subject to any state laws "to the extent not inconsistent with [Title I of ERISA]."[50]

On the face of it, the law seemed clear. States would maintain the same regulatory authority over MEWAS as they did over licensed insurers, except for fully insured MEWAS, over which they had limited authority. Given that most of the problems had occurred with self-funded METS, the 1983 amendments to ERISA seemed to resolve the problems. However, numerous ambiguities remained in interpreting the amended language. These ambiguities produced considerable confusion among the states about their regulatory authority over MEWAS and created the loopholes that would allow for massive fraud in the industry.

First, under the Erlenborn amendments, ERISA allowed the Department of Labor (DOL) to grant exemptions from state regulation to MEWAS "individually or by class."[51] Despite the fact that as of 1992 the Department of Labor had granted no such exemptions,[52] this legal loophole allowed the operators of fraudulent MEWAS, when confronted by state regulators who questioned their ERISA status, to claim that they were in the process of applying to the Department of Labor for an exemption. More generally, state insurance regulators complained that the Department of Labor did not maintain a program for certifying ERISA plans. All the law required was that ERISA plans file a financial statement with the Department within 19 months after going into business.[53] Even then, the Department did not conduct an audit of the organization to verify its ERISA preemption claim, but rather would offer "opinions" on individual claims only after being requested to do so by state insurance departments. It would often take many months for them to respond to such a request, and their response was often vague. In the intervening period, MEWA crooks could continue to run their operations, collecting premiums for future claims that they never intended to pay, while state regulators were unable to shut them down as "unauthorized insurers" because of the uncertainty of their ERISA status.[54]

Second, it was not clear what the phrase "not inconsistent with Title I" meant in practical terms. Did it mean, for example, that states had the authority to license self-funded MEWAS the same way they did insurance companies? Could they require MEWAs to contribute to state guaranty funds? For many state regulators, the answers were not clear.[55]

Finally, even where the provisions in ERISA are clear regarding state regulation, fraudulent MEWA operators have been able to confound state regulators by simply claiming to be fully funded by licensed insurance carriers when they were in fact self-funded. Attempts by poorly staffed state regulators to shut down fraudulent MEWAs were often delayed for months as they attempted to backtrack through a maze of documents presented by MEWA operators purporting to show that their plans were backed by legitimate insurers.[56]

Employee Leasing Scams

In addition to fraudulent MEWAs, white-collar criminals have used the ambiguities in ERISA to defraud health insurance consumers by using other scams, one of which involves *employee leasing organizations.* Under these arrangements, individual employers "fire" their employees, who are then "hired" by an employee leasing firm that provides insurance, payroll, and other services to the employers. By pooling the employees of numerous companies, the leasing firm has a large enough number of employees, on paper, to qualify for lower group rates. While some of these arrangements are legitimate, the insurance obtained by the leasing company

is often unsound or non-existent, consisting [of] nothing more than an in-house, unauthorized, self-insurance scheme in which the staff leasing company pays yesterday's claims with today's insurance premiums, creating yet another "Ponzi" scheme that ultimately collapses, leaving thousands of workers without health or compensation benefits.[57]

Many of these fraudulent leasing firms claim to be self- or fully funded, single employer benefit plans and thus exempt from state regulations under the provisions of ERISA. Despite the fact that their "employees" work at different sites and for different managements, technically they are still employed by the leasing firm. Only after a number of leasing firms failed to pay medical claims did the courts and the Department of Labor begin handing down rulings and opinions to clarify the issue. As we shall see in later chapters, lack of clarity surrounding this issue created a gaping loophole in regulatory laws that enabled operators of corrupt leasing organizations to scam thousands of employees and employers out of their earnings.

Bogus Labor Unions

Possibly even more vexing for regulators have been illegal schemes that take advantage of ERISA language regarding health plans offered by labor unions. Recall that under the original provisions of ERISA, "any plan or arrangement which is established or maintained (i) under or pursuant to one or more agreements which the Secretary [of the Department of Labor] finds to be collective bargaining agreements" is not considered a MEWA and is exempted fully from state regulation. This provision was intended to allow labor unions to offer health plans to their members at the affordable prices paid by the employees of large corporations that self-insure. In effect, it means that health plans offered by labor unions are exempt from all state regulations and are subject to no comparable federal regulatory standards.[58]

Beginning in the late 1980s, a number of entrepreneurs saw in this obscure provision a means for perpetrating massive insurance frauds. Federal law does not define what a valid union organization is and therefore what constitutes an "employee welfare plan" that has been "collectively bargained." In some instances, the operators would simply gain control over a dormant union that was originally established for legitimate purposes and would then market health plans to "associate members," persons unrelated by occupation or employment. In other cases, insurance crooks would create new unions. It turns out to be remarkably easy for anyone to start a labor union. All it takes is the filing of several documents with the

Department of Labor.[59] Once established, these "unions" are able to market health care plans to prospective "members" with sales pitches that emphasize the cost benefits resulting from their exemption from state regulation.

State regulators have discovered that the expedient closure of these sham unions is exceedingly difficult. When confronted, the operators claim an ERISA preemption that prohibits state officials from investigating their plans. While regulators have been generally successful in convincing judges that these plans are not valid ERISA plans and in obtaining cease and desist orders, the process of going through the courts often proves time-consuming, allowing the operators time to continue collecting premiums from unsuspecting employers and employees. Even after injunctions are obtained in one state, the crooks often simply move their operations to another state.

IN SUMMARY, the passage of ERISA in 1974 and the Erlenborn amendments in 1983 were intended to expand the availability of health insurance to the employees of small businesses and other groups (1) by recognizing the legality of nontraditional insurance providers, and (2) by giving those providers the edge they needed to market affordable insurance plans by exempting them from some of the state regulations applicable to traditional insurance companies.

While these groups were not exempt from all state regulation—fully insured MEWAs were governed by state laws regarding reserves, for example—they were not subject to a number of state regulations, including licensing and the regular submission of financial statements. Most fraudulent health plans are *not* valid ERISA plans under any of the above definitions but are simply unauthorized insurers who hide behind claims that they are protected by ERISA. If it were not for these claims, state regulators could quickly shut them down with cease and desist orders. A critical gap in the law was that it did not require that the Department of Labor certify a plan as an authorized ERISA plan *before* it was marketed to employers.

Combined with the fact that the Department had (at best) an inefficient mechanism in place for determining ERISA status on an ad hoc basis, this left state regulators in the dark about the ERISA status of suspect health insurance plans operating in their states until it was too late.[60] Thus, in the hands of the "financial knaves and buccaneers"[61] who prospered in the black market of the health insurance industry, ERISA functioned as a "tactical legal weapon"[62] in their fight to ward off government oversight of their activities.

CONCLUSIONS

As the preceding discussion indicates, fraud in the small business health insurance industry is a complicated issue, largely because of the significant impacts that industry changes and regulatory laws have had on the market. The result has been a criminogenic market in which the "nature of transactions"[63] and the regulatory environment in which the market functions have created tremendous opportunities for white-collar criminals to siphon off millions of dollars from bogus insurance plans. In some ways the situation is similar to the savings and loan crisis of the 1980s in which deregulatory laws, enacted in the early part of the decade in an effort to save an industry that had been battered by rising interest rates, had the unintended consequence of leaving the door open for widespread fraud and abuse, resulting in billions of dollars in losses.[64] In the case of the small group health insurance industry, federal laws that sought to respond to market conditions by deregulating a portion of the market—by allowing nontraditional insurers to offer plans outside of state regulatory mechanisms—had a similar effect by creating a "twilight world somewhere between State and Federal regulation"[65] in which white-collar criminals could prosper. The sources of both crises are similar and, as later chapters shall argue, reveal structural weaknesses in regulatory systems that are found in related areas of insurance and other financial industries.[66]

NOTES

1 Remarkably, a number of Republican leaders argued that the "health care crisis" was a myth, a scare tactic on the part of Democratic backers of the Clinton health care proposal. Senate Minority Leader Bob Dole stated that America's health care system had "serious problems," but that they did not represent a "crisis." Guy Molyneux, " 'Crisis? What Crisis?'—The GOP Respond to the Health-Care Issue Politics," *Los Angeles Times,* 30 January 1994, p. 1.

2 In the 1980s and early 1990s, inflation-adjusted data on health care expenditures show annual increases that averaged between 6 and 8 percent. Katharine Levit, Helen Lazenby, and Lekha Sivarajan, "Health Care Spending in 1994," *Health Affairs* 15 (2): 132 (1996).

3 House Committee on Energy and Commerce, Subcommittee on Health and the Environment, *Small Business Health Insurance Market,* 101st Cong., 1st sess., 16 October 1989, 6–8.

4 Today there is no federal regulation over the industry. This policy was affirmed with the passage of the McCarran-Ferguson Act in 1945. The law temporarily exempted insurance companies from certain antitrust laws and declared that the regulation of the insurance industry would remain under the jurisdiction of individual states. The McCarran-Ferguson Act was a legislative response to a Supreme Court case decided a year earlier in which the Court ruled that insurance was commerce and therefore subject to federal antitrust restrictions. The Supreme Court case emerged out of an earlier case in which the Attorney General of Missouri had indicted officers and executives at 200 fire insurance companies on charges they had conspired to fix insurance rates. Kenneth Meir, *The Political Economy of Regulation: The Case of Insurance* (Albany: State University of New York Press, 1988), 64–70.

5 General Accounting Office, *Health Insurance: Cost Increases Lead to Coverage Limitations and Cost Shifting,* GAO/HRD-90-68, May 1990, p. 21.

6 House Committee on Ways and Means, Subcommittee on Health, *Private Health Insurance: Options for Reform,* 101st Cong., 2d sess., 20 September 1990, 12.

7 Health maintenance organizations (HMOs) are "organizations that provide services to an enrolled population for a fixed, prepaid, per capita fee." Preferred provider organizations (PPOs) are "networks of medical providers who charge on a fee-for-service basis, but are paid on a negotiated, discounted fee schedule." Lynn Bremmer, *Handbook for Reporters* (New York: Insurance Information Institute, 1993), 47–48.

8 House Committee on Energy and Commerce, Subcommittee on Health and the Environment, *Small Business Health Insurance Market,* 101st Cong., 1st sess., 16 October 1989, 34.

9 U.S. Department of Health and Human Services, *Health, United States, 1994* (Washington, D.C.: GPO, 1995), 39.

10 House Committee, *Small Business Health Insurance Market,* 34.

11 General Accounting Office, *Employment-Based Health Insurance: Costs Increase and Family Coverage Decreases,* GAO/HEHS-97-35, February 1997.

12 Underwriting refers to the "selecting and rating of risks that are presented to an insurer." House Committee, *Private Health Insurance: Options for Reform,* 10. Underwriting practices determine who is considered eligible for health insurance and the amount that individuals will be required to pay in the form of premiums for coverage.

   The term actually originated with Lloyds of London in the seventeenth century. The firm's founder, a London coffee shop owner named Edward Lloyd, had patrons of his shop sign their names, one below the other, at the bottom of each policy—hence the term *underwriting.* James Trager, *The People's Chronology* (New York: Henry Holt, 1995), 264.

13 Congressional Research Service, *Insuring the Uninsured* (Washington, D.C.: GPO, 1988), 21.

14 Milt Freudenheim, "Health Insurers' Changing Role," *New York Times,* 16 January 1990, p. D2; Eric Berg, "Insurance Giants No Longer Ask to Be All Things to All People," *New York Times,* 7 February 1991, p. A1; Joseph Crowley, "Where Have All the Players Gone?" *Best's Review,* April 1989, pp. 46–107.

15 W. K. Zellers, C. G. McLaughlin, and K. D. Frick, "Small-Business Health Insurance: Only the Healthy Need Apply," *Health Affairs* (Spring 1992): 179.

16 GAO, *Employment-Based Health Insurance,* 29–31.

17 Milt Freudenheim, "Health Insurers, to Reduce Losses, Blacklist Dozens of Occupations," *New York Times,* 5 February 1990, p. A1.

18 Ibid.; Kathleen Day, "Health Insurers' Catch-22: The Ill Need Not Apply," *Washington Post,* 4 October 1992, p. H1.

19 Ibid.

20 House Committee, *Private Health Insurance: Options for Reform,* 8.

21 Jeanne Saddler, "Cheaper Health Insurance for Small Firms Carries Catch," *Wall Street Journal,* 30 October 1989, p. B2.

22 House Committee, *Small Business Health Insurance Market,* 35.

23 House Subcommittee on Oversight and Investigations, Committee on Energy and Commerce, *Health Insurance Industry Practices,* statement of Cathy Hurwit, Legislative Director, Citizen Action, 103d Cong., 2d sess., 29 June and 3 August 1994, 368.

24 Brian Kelley, "National Debate Gets Personal," *Roanoke Times & World News,* 21 January 1994, p. 1; Brian Kelley, "Insurance Will Cover Surgery After All," *Roanoke Times & World News,* 17 February 1994, p. N-4.

25 Leslie Scism, "Picking Cherries: Health Insurer Profits by Being Very Choosy in Selling its Policies," *Wall Street Journal,* 20 September 1994, p. A1.

26 Ibid.

27 House Subcommittee on Oversight and Investigations, Committee on Energy and Commerce, *Health Insurance Industry Practices,* 103d Cong., 2d sess., 29 June and 3 August 1994, 373–74.

28 Ibid., 9.

29 Ibid., 38–39.

30 Ibid., 55.

31 Clay Chandler, "Favored Few Stand to Gain from Republican Tax Cuts," *Washington Post,* 24 December 1995, p. A1.

32 House Committee on Ways and Means, *Overview of Entitlement Programs: 1991 Green Book,* 102d Cong., 1st Sess., 7 May 1991, 313; Employee Benefit Research Institute, *Sources of Health Insurance and Characteristics of the Uninsured* (Washington, D.C.: Employee Benefit Research Institute, 1996), 1.

33 Employee Benefit Research Institute, *Sources of Health Insurance,* 6.

34 The Pepper Commission, U.S. Bipartisan Commission on Comprehensive Health Care, *A Call for Action,* final report, September 1990, 25.

35 W. David Helms, Anne Gauthier, and Daniel Campion, "Mending the Flaws in the Small-Group Market," *Health Affairs* (Summer 1992): 7–27.

36 For a discussion of the concept of "organizational weapons," see Stanton Wheeler and Mitchell Rothman, "The Organization as Weapon in White Collar Crime," *Michigan Law Review* 80 (1982): 1403–26.

37 One of the best-known pension fund catastrophes occurred in 1964, when the Studebaker automobile company closed down a plant in South Bend, Indiana. Because the firm's pension fund lacked sufficient assets, some 4,500 workers lost 85 percent of their vested benefits. *Congressional Record,* 93d Cong., 1st sess., 19 (18 September 1993), p. 30003.

38 The overwhelming emphasis in ERISA was on pension plans. Out of the several thousand pages of conference hearings on ERISA, only five were devoted to the discussion of health care plans. Senate Committee on Labor and Human Resources, *Employer Group Purchasing Reform Act of 1995,* 104th Cong., 1st sess., 25 July 1995, 1.

39 29 U.S.C. § 1002(1) (1983).

40 29 U.S.C. § 1114(a)514(b)(2)(B) (1975).

41 Under ERISA, insurers with over 100 participants must file a "summary plan description" that includes "the source of financing of the plan and the identity of any organization through which benefits are provided" to the Department of Labor within 120 days of the inception of the plan. Plan operators are also required to submit annual reports, which include financial statements (Form 5500), with the Department of Labor and the Internal Revenue Service within 210 days after the close of the first year in which the plan is in operation. 29 U.S.C. § 1023(1) (1975).

ERISA also requires that these annual financial statements (for employee benefit plans with over 100 participants) be reviewed by an independent public accountant (IPA). The quality of these documents and the Department of Labor's review of them, however, have come under considerable criticism. An examination of 279 IPA reports chosen at random by the Department of Labor's Office of the Inspector General [OIG] found that nearly two-thirds (65 percent) of them "did not meet ERISA or DOL requirements." House Select Committee on Aging, Subcommittee on Retirement Income and Employment, *Who's Minding Your Pension?* 101st Cong., 1st sess., 15 November 1989, 157–59. Moreover, as Congressman Hughes pointed out in hearings on the subject in 1989:

> Independent Public Accountant auditors are not required to directly report violations they find in the pension plans to the PWBA, which is responsible for enforcing ERISA provisions. Rather, the auditors report their findings to the plan administrators who, in turn, are often supposed to report violations of their own activities. Ibid., 2.

In 1995, the OIG conducted a follow-up study using a similar methodology. The study assessed the quality of 262 IPA audits of employee benefit plans that were done in 1992, of which 53 were "health and welfare plans." Of the audits examined, 33 failed to "comply with one or more of ERISA's reporting requirements." U.S. Department of Labor, Pension and Welfare Benefits Administration, *Assessment of the Quality of Employee Benefit Plans,* draft report, 29 May 1996, 27.

42 House Committee on Education and Labor, Subcommittee on Labor-Management Relations, *Oversight Investigation of Certain Multiple Employer Health Insurance Trusts (METs), Evading State and Federal Regulation,* 97th Cong., 2d sess., 5 March 1982.

43 Ibid., 4–9.

44 Ibid., 8.

45 House Committee, *Oversight Investigation.*

46 Multiple Employer Welfare Act of 1982, 29 U.S.C. § 1002(1) (1983).

47 29 U.S.C. § 1002(40)(A) (1983).

48 Steven Cassidy, "Multiple Employer Trusts: From ERISA to the Present," *Journal of American Society of CLU,* March 1987, p. 62.

49 29 U.S.C. § 1144(6)(A)(i)(I) (1983). Here the word *contributions* refers to what are commonly referred to as *premiums* in traditional health care plans.

50 29 U.S.C. § 1144(6)(A)(ii) (1983).

51 29 U.S.C. § 1144(6)(B)(A)(ii) (1983).

52 U.S. Department of Labor, Pension and Welfare Benefits Administration, MEWAs, *Multiple Employer Welfare Arrangements Under the Employee Retirement Income Security Act: A Guide to Federal and State Regulation,* 1992, 41.

53 See note 41 *supra.*

54 Senate Committee on Governmental Affairs, Permanent Subcommittee on Investigations, *U.S. Government Efforts to Combat Fraud and Abuse in the Insurance Industry,* 102d Cong., 2d sess., Report 102-262, 12 March 1992, 10–12; Senate Committee on Governmental Affairs, Permanent Subcommittee on Investigations, *Fraud and Abuse in Employer Sponsored Health Benefit Plans,* testimony of Jo Ann Howard, Texas State Board of Insurance, 101st Cong., 2d sess., 15 May 1990, 126–27.

55 House Select Committee on Aging, Subcommittee on Retirement Income and Employment, *Small Businesses and Older Workers Health Benefits: Multiple Employer Welfare Arrangements, The Problem or the Solution,* 102d Cong., 1st sess., 17 September 1991, 128.

56 Ibid., 123.

57 Travis County, Texas, District Attorney's Office, "Travis County District Attorney's Office, Insurance Fraud Section, Report on Insurance Fraud," 16 February 1993, 14–15.

58 The Taft-Hartley Act of 1947 gave formal recognition to union health plans as part of collective bargaining agreements. (Pub. L. No. 101, § 302(c)(5).

59 Federal regulations require that "labor organizations" submit a written constitution with a set of bylaws and a brief form (DOL-LM-1) listing the name of the union and its officers and other information within 90 days of being organized. Thereafter, the organization is required to submit annual financial reports with the Department of Labor. 29 C.F.R. pts. 402–403.

60 House Committee, *Who's Minding Your Pension?* 114–15.

61 House Committee on Energy and Commerce, Subcommittee on Oversight and Investigations, *Failed Promises: Insurance Company Insolvencies,* 101st Cong., 2d sess., February 1990, 3.

62 Senate Committee, *U.S. Government Efforts to Combat,* 9.

63 Diane Vaughan, *Controlling Unlawful Organizational Behavior* (Chicago: University of Chicago Press, 1983), 6.

64 Kitty Calavita, Henry Pontell, and Robert Tillman, *Big Money Crime: Fraud and Politics in the Savings and Loan Crisis* (Berkeley: University of California Press, 1997), 9–16.

65 Senate Committee, *Fraud and Abuse in Employer Sponsored Health Benefit Plans,* opening statement of Sen. Sam Nunn, 3.

66 The parallels between the savings and loan crisis and insider fraud in employee welfare plans were made explicit by the Office of the Inspector General, Department of Labor, in 1989. In its semiannual report, the OIG noted that in the recently discovered savings and loan crisis, financial auditors had failed to adequately report on problems at failed savings and loans and stated that "an unknown portion of the $1.6 trillion in assets that are currently in private pension plans likewise may be at risk, for many of the same reasons. . . . Unless steps are taken now, today's S&L bail-out may become tomorrow's ERISA nightmare." U.S. Department of Labor, Office of the Inspector General, *Semiannual Report, October 1, 1988–March 31, 1989* (Washington, D.C.: GPO, 1989), 3. Though these comments were directed largely at the vulnerability of pension plans, the Inspector General was referring to "employee benefit plans" generally, including health insurance plans.

The Trouble with MEWAs

O N May 15, 1990, sixteen years after the passage of the Employee Retirement Income Security Act (ERISA), Sen. Sam Nunn of Georgia announced the opening of congressional hearings on fraud in the multiple employer welfare arrangement (MEWA) industry with a sense of urgency: "Unscrupulous [MEWA] promoters . . . are literally playing with people's lives."[1] Nearly two years later, after the hearings were finished, Senator Nunn's committee issued a report that concluded:

For almost 18 years now, conmen, crooks and hucksters have been able to take advantage of a continuing regulatory vacuum (be it actual or perceived) in the area of self-insured employer sponsored health benefit programs to fleece unsuspecting employers and their employees of hard-earned premium dollars. They have built their lavish lifestyles on the shattered lives of innocent men, women and children while regulators have argued with one another over who has jurisdiction and whether the problem has already been solved.[2]

This chapter describes some of these "conmen, crooks and hucksters," their schemes and their victims. At their root, all were Ponzi schemes in which large amounts of money was collected from unsuspecting individuals with promises to pay their future medical expenses. Early claims were paid from the pool of incoming premiums, but later claims were never paid as the money had been siphoned off and the plans collapsed. As we shall see, MEWAS provided ideal vehicles for these scams because their exemption from state regulatory laws allowed these "unscrupulous promoters" to set them up with no initial capital investment and without providing any evidence of their plans' financial soundness. All that was required was clever salesmanship.

MET PROBLEMS BECOME MEWA PROBLEMS

During the late 1970s and early 1980s, many multiple employer trusts (METs) failed, leaving millions of dollars in unpaid claims.[3] In California alone, between 1977 and 1983, 47 METs became insolvent.[4] The largest of these failures was a MET known as the American Benefit Ltd. Trust (ABL). Between 1979 and 1982, when it was shut down by regulators, ABL enrolled 70,000 employees in its health plan, generating premium payments of up to $4 million a month. The plan failed because 40 percent of those premiums were used to pay commissions and administrative costs, a percentage that far exceeded the amount found in legitimate insurance companies. When it failed, ABL had only $350,000 in assets to cover an estimated $4 million in unpaid claims.[5]

Many bogus METs and MEWAS have targeted ministers and other employees of religious organizations. In 1978, four years after ERISA was enacted, Bob E. Browning, a wealthy, "born again" Texas businessman, began selling health insurance, sponsored by his Ministers Benefit Trust (MBT), to clergy and other church employees around the country. Browning claimed that MBT was an ERISA trust and therefore not required to meet state-mandated capital requirements. From the beginning, the trust was actuarially unsound and would eventually leave some 250 pastors with unpaid medical bills totaling an estimated $300,000. The trust was temporarily rescued in 1979 when Browning negotiated with well-known televangelist Jerry Falwell to have 500 employees from Falwell's *Old Time Gospel Hour* television program receive health benefits from the trust. When MBT was declared insolvent and was shut down by the state of Texas in 1980, critics pointed out that Falwell's employees had their claims paid while other policyholders were left high and dry. Browning's detractors claimed that the situation was the result of an agreement between Browning and Falwell in which Browning received a $50,000 contract to study the feasibility of constructing a building for Falwell's organization and in exchange, Falwell's employees would receive priority over other policyholders.[6]

Browning apparently was not too dispirited by the closure of MBT, for just two years later he created a new organization called the Christians Organizations Medical Society, Inc., which sold health insurance to churches and ministry organizations. In 1985, the Texas Board of Insurance shut the organization down, after amassing a foot-thick file of complaints from dissatisfied customers who, collectively, were left with an estimated $4.7 million in unpaid claims. In 1990, Browning was convicted in federal court on charges of mail fraud in connection with the organization and was sentenced to serve 15 years in prison.[7]

Legislators attempted to fill the legal loopholes in ERISA with the passage of the Erlenborn amendments in 1983. But soon thereafter it became clear that all that had happened was that "MET problems had become MEWA problems"[8] and that, if anything, the schemes had become grander and the losses greater. One case garnered considerable public attention because it seemed to represent everything that was wrong with MEWAS and MEWA regulation. The case involved two partners, Michael Rubell and James Helm, who set up an elaborate multistate operation that took advantage of the intense demand by small businesses for affordable insurance to perpetrate a massive fraud.

RUBELL-HELM

The modus operandi of Rubell and Helm's schemes was straightforward and was repeated numerous times in different states. They would target groups of policyholders who were about to lose their insurance or organizations in need of insurance for their members and then offer to provide health insurance benefits to employees who contributed to a trust fund managed by Rubell-Helm Insurance Services (RHIS). These premiums purportedly would be used to purchase insurance and to cover administrative costs. After taking in thousands of dollars in premiums from the new enrollees and paying off some of their initial claims, they would then begin slow-paying later claims and eventually stop payments altogether. Operating through these schemes, Rubell-Helm and their associates were able to take in millions of dollars in premiums in only a couple of years.

In 1986, RHIS contracted with Longwood Management Corp., which operated a string of nursing homes in California, to provide health insurance to its employees. By early 1988, complaints were coming into Longwood's offices at an average of 12 per day from employees and physicians claiming that their bills were not being paid. After getting the runaround from RHIS employees, Longwood executives demanded that the MEWA hand over its records to an outside claims administrator they had hired to clean up the mess. When they finally got the records they found boxes stuffed with files containing unpaid claims totaling $450,000.[9]

In the fall of 1987, the California Association of Builders Exchange (CABE), an employers' association that represented building contractors throughout the state, hired RHIS to design and administer a fully insured health plan for its members. Initially, RHIS was able to persuade a legitimate insurance company, Boston Mutual, to provide stop-loss insurance for the CABE plan. But within months Boston Mutual canceled the policy. RHIS then explained to CABE trustees that the health plan would thereafter be a self-funded ERISA plan with reinsurance supplied by an offshore insurer. In fact, no such insurance had been purchased. Rubell and Helm were assisted in their scheme by the chairman of the CABE trustees, David Erlandson, whom they bribed with secret payments totaling $24,500.[10]

In February 1988, the Diamond Benefits Life Insurance Company (a licensed insurer) informed employers enrolled in its Diamond Care plan in California and Florida that it was terminating their life and health insurance coverage as of April of that year. Soon thereafter, many of those employers received letters from RHIS that offered them a new plan, the American Insurance Trust Plan, with the same benefits as Diamond Care. With the aid of an executive at Diamond Life, whom they bribed with a payment of $50,000, they were able to persuade employers who signed up that Diamond Life fully insured the new plan, though now it would be administered by RHIS. In July, they made a similar pitch to employers enrolled in the Florida Retail Federation Association Good Health Trust, whom had recently been informed that their coverage was being canceled.[11] Operating through CABE and the American Insurance Trust Plan, Rubell and Helm were able to enroll approximately 4,000 Floridians in their MEWAS.[12]

In Texas, RHIS marketed its plans through an entity called the National Family Business Association (NFBA), which ostensibly provided health plans to family businesses. Apparently, RHIS's definition of a *family* business was quite broad since they enrolled employees of school districts, housing authorities, and county governments. Eventually they were able to take in $700,000 from Texas employees. When they finally were shut down in the state, they left at least $300,000 in unpaid claims.[13]

In the spring of 1988 RHIS contracted with Tulare County, California, officials to provide health benefits to several hundred of the county's employees. The firm entered into a similar agreement with a builders' association in the county. In both cases, Rubell, Helm, and their associates misled those they contracted with into believing that they were providing legitimate benefits backed with stop-loss insurance they were purchasing with portions of the premiums sent to them by employees. They were instead simply pocketing the money.

Federal authorities later estimated that during their short-lived involvement in the MEWA industry, Rubell, Helm, and their associates misappropriated millions of dollars. They embezzled $1.6 million from the funds of American Insurance Trust Plan alone.[14] Their crimes left an estimated $10.4 million in medical and life insurance claims unpaid.

Instead of paying the medical claims for the thousands of workers who had diligently sent in their premiums, they used these monies to support extravagant lifestyles. Investigators later learned that RHIS expenditures included:

- $1 million used by Helm's wife, who was also involved in the schemes, to renovate and remodel a ranch house in Colorado, to pay for Caribbean vacations, and to purchase clothing and jewelry;[15]

- $500,000 used by Rubell to pay for a condominium at a ski resort, diamonds, and the services of a maid and a personal trainer;[16]

- $100,000 to $200,000 used by Helm to pay a well-known Southern California clothier for custom clothing, including $1,500 suits and $300 pairs of shoes;[17]

- $2,600 and $2,000 a month to pay the respective salaries of Rubell's housekeeper and Helm's mother-in-law, neither of whom, according to the former controller at RHIS, performed any work in exchange for their salaries;[18]

- $500 a week for three years to pay a psychiatrist who was treating Rubell's son;[19]

- $12,000 for a Caribbean vacation for Rubell;[20]

- undisclosed amounts to pay for leased cars for RHIS employees, including a Range Rover for Helm and a Chevy Suburban and an Audi for his wife.[21]

Meanwhile, the people who had sent in their monthly premiums to RHIS and assumed their health care expenses were covered were not doing so well. One of RHIS's victims was Donald Smith, an Arizona paint contractor. After the insurance premiums he was paying to a licensed insurance company for medical benefits for himself and his employees increased dramatically, Smith decided to look for less expensive options. Unfortunately, he found RHIS through CABE and took out a policy. Soon thereafter his wife developed a terminal illness that resulted in medical bills of over $80,000. RHIS never paid any of them. In testimony before a congressional committee in 1991, Smith explained his situation. Faced with his wife's monthly medical bills of $400 to $500, he was considering taking a minimum wage job just to obtain health care benefits for his wife, though, he added grimly, "there is a possibility that my wife will die within a year's time and then I won't have the problem."[22]

Another one of RHIS's victims was Janet Robinson,[23] an office manager for a small company that was a member of CABE. In March 1988, her employer began making premium payments for Robinson to RHIS's life and health insurance plans. That summer, Robinson experienced a recurrence of cancer that had been in remission. After undergoing extensive treatments, she discovered that RHIS was not paying her medical bills. The insurance agent who signed up her employer in the plan tried in vain to persuade RHIS to pay her claims. In May 1989, Robinson succumbed to her illness. In a final letter to Helm, president of RHIS, the agent wrote:

Up until the time of her [Robinson's] death, she was harassed by creditors trying to collect those claims, which you had promised to pay last October, but never did. She went to her deathbed being agonized by the fact that she left thousands of dollars of debt through no fault of her own. *I don't know if you have any con-science whatsoever, but if you do, I wanted to make you aware of the living horror that you are putting people through because of your past activities.*[24] (Emphasis added.)

RHIS's victim list also includes Janet Parker,[25] a mother of two boys from Baton Rouge, Louisiana. In 1988, her em-ployer, a small social service agency in Baton Rouge, enrolled its employees in the CABE health plan, and Parker felt confi-dent that her family's medical needs were taken care of. Her confidence was shattered when she learned that RHIS was not paying her claims. In one instance, her oldest son had an acci-dent resulting in a torn cornea. The bill from the surgeon who repaired her son's eye was $2,900. RHIS ignored the claim she submitted for the bill. Afterwards, Parker did not take her son in for postoperative follow-up care "because I knew that Rubell Helm would not pay the claim and I was not able to pay the cost myself."

Later, RHIS refused to pay a bill for $3,411 when her son was hospitalized for an asthma attack. Again, she decided to forgo treatment for her children. In her own words:

I knew that claims I had made to Rubell Helm were not being paid. I therefore delayed seeking medical care and hospitalization for both my sons when they were having asthma attacks, even though I knew that both my sons needed professional medical care and atten-tion. I would have hospitalized my sons during those attacks, but I believed that if I could get my sons through one night at a time, that I could save the cost of hospitalization and the embarrassment I felt when dealing with the hospital administrators. I will never forget how anxious I was when caring for my sick children.[26]

The experiences of these victims reveal that the crimes com-mitted by Rubell, Helm, and their associates did not simply result in monetary losses but inflicted pain and physical harm on their victims.

Things began to unravel quickly for Rubell and Helm in early 1989. In February, the Florida Department of Insurance issued a cease and desist order against RHIS and related entities.[27] In March, the California Department of Insurance announced it was seeking to revoke their agents' licenses and was investigating the firm for wrongdoing.[28] In June, the state of Texas obtained a temporary restraining order against the firm.[29] At Senator Nunn's hearings held in May, RHIS was featured as an example of the problems in the MEWA industry.[30] Then, in August 1991, Rubell and Helm's wife Kathleen were indicted by federal prosecutors in southern California. Rubell almost immediately entered a guilty plea and was sentenced to serve 30 months in prison. In 1993, Helm and two former RHIS executives were indicted. Helm was eventually convicted and sentenced to four years in prison.

LEGAL WEAPONRY

A key element in many MEWA scams has been the deployment of attorneys who respond to regulators' attempts to shut down their client's organization with a flurry of suits and counter-suits challenging the jurisdiction of state officials over ERISA plans. As regulatory agencies, state insurance departments cannot initiate criminal prosecution but instead rely on civil and administrative actions, such as cease and desist orders or temporary restraining orders issued by judges. These orders can be challenged, and while they are being sorted out in court, the plaintiffs can continue marketing their health insurance plans and raking in premiums. Texas officials described the obstacles that such protracted litigation created for regulators:

The promoters of self-funded MEWAs typically are prepared to fight out in court the twin issues of documentation and regulatory status. Money rightfully belonging to policyholders is plowed into attorney fees, expert witness fees, discovery fees, court costs, travel expenses and the like. The attraction of maintaining a continuing stream of contribution dollars during protracted litigation far exceeds the cost and nuisance of going to court. The value of clever lawyers is illustrated by an alleged agreement by one MEWA to pay its attorney a fixed percentage of contributions received. Meanwhile, the various state attorneys general and the overburdened judicial system have limited resources, upon which many other demands are made. As a result, it is difficult to obtain speedy judgements in civil litigation against promoters of illegal MEWAS.[31]

Crooked MEWA operators learned quickly that ERISA could serve them well as a "tactical legal weapon"[32] in their battles with regulators. Among those who learned this lesson well were the operators of a Texas-based MEWA known as the International Association of Entrepreneurs of America (IAEA). Founded in 1992 as a spinoff from a fraudulent labor union (see Chapter 4 for more details), IAEA went on to sign up clients for its health and workers' compensation plans in 29 states. Insurance regulators in many of those states attempted to shut down the MEWA, and IAEA's officials responded with civil suits filed in state and federal courts asserting federal preemption from state regulation. By the spring of 1995, IAEA had been involved in legal battles in Colorado, Illinois, Maine, Minnesota, Missouri, Texas, and Virginia.[33] In Missouri, state regulators obtained a temporary restraining order against IAEA in 1994, but that order was stayed pending an appeal. Eventually the case wound up in a federal appeals court where a judge ruled in favor of the Missouri Department of Insurance, but in the meantime IAEA had continued taking in premiums and failing to pay medical claims.[34] It was not until 1996, when a federal judge froze the MEWA's assets, that IAEA was shut down permanently.

The use of legal tactics to delay state intervention in the activities of fraudulent medical plans was central to the strategy of another MEWA operator, an aspiring rock musician named Edward Zinner.

A ROCK AND ROLL LEGEND [35]

On January 17, 1991, Edward Zinner, a 31-year-old Virginian, and his business partner, William Moulton, filed papers incorporating the United Healthcare Association, a multiple employer welfare arrangement, in Virginia Beach, Virginia.[36] Zinner had met Moulton the previous year when they both worked for a California MEWA run by Hameed "Tony" Ullah. In that year, Ullah had successfully resisted an attempt by California regulators to shut down his operation by obtaining a temporary restraining order in federal court. Seeing his former employer's success, Zinner decided to strike out on his own and create his own MEWA. However, having recently declared bankruptcy, he lacked money. This is where Moulton entered the picture. Moulton, who had been in the insurance business since 1963, had several things that Zinner needed: a dormant Virginia corporation called National Insurance Consultants (NIC), an office building and equipment, and $1,500. Together with $1,500 from Zinner, this was enough to allow the pair to create a MEWA that would eventually pull in millions of dollars in premiums.

The United Healthcare Association was purported to be an association of small employers and self-employed individuals that offered a health plan, known as the Atlantic Plan, to its members. Benefits were to be provided through the Atlantic Healthcare Benefits Trust (AHBT), which Zinner would control through several straw trustees. NIC was the third-party administrator that would handle claims for the Atlantic Plan. NIC, which was also controlled by Zinner, marketed the plan across the country through a network of brokers and agents.

At meetings with agents and sales representatives Zinner would claim that the trust was fully insured and that reinsurance was being provided by Lloyds of London. He would also tell agents that the association was financially rock solid with $5 million in assets. To bolster their confidence, at a March 1991 meeting with agents, Zinner introduced as a Lloyds representative a man who was in fact a broker with NIC.

Almost from their inception the Atlantic Plan and the United Healthcare Association ran into problems with state insurance regulators, who by the beginning of 1991 had become aware of the potential dangers with MEWAs. In March, Maryland issued a cease and desist order against Zinner that prohibited him from marketing the Atlantic Plan in the state. State officials were concerned about the real level of reserves backing the plan. At a hearing before the state insurance bureau in June, Zinner testified that he had found an "investor" who, via a holding company, had transferred $5 million to the plan and that "we have more than the required capital and surplus to form an insurance company that is required in any state."[37] Despite this claim, Maryland affirmed the cease and desist order, but allowed Zinner to continue selling his products in the state pending an appeal of the decision. Meanwhile, in April, Zinner's home state of Virginia hit him with a cease and desist order after discovering that Atlantic Trust's assets consisted of only $11,000 in a bank account.

In December 1991, Connecticut informed Zinner that state insurance regulators were investigating Atlantic and requested information regarding the plan's finances. Zinner refused to provide the information and filed suit against the commissioner of the state insurance department in federal court. In that suit, Zinner and colleagues claimed that as a bona fide MEWA, Atlantic was not subject to state regulations and thus was not required to provide any information to Connecticut officials. They pointed to an opinion from the Department of Labor that stated that Atlantic did meet the federal criteria for MEWAS.[38] Nonetheless, a federal appellate court eventually upheld a lower court ruling that even if Atlantic was a MEWA, it could still be subject to limited state regulation under ERISA guidelines.[39]

The amount of capital held in reserve by the plan was a constant source of conflicting information, even within the organization. Zinner bragged to employees that he and Moulton had started the organization with $3,000 and an office. A marketing executive who had been hired at the plan's inception was initially told by Zinner that there was $300,000 set aside to cover expenses. When the executive later questioned this amount, Zinner told him that the "300,000" was actually 300,000 pennies.

Zinner told regulators in a number of states as well as employees of United and agents who marketed the plan that the Atlantic Plan was backed by $4.5 million in reserves. Yet, there were always shifting explanations about where the $4.5 million was coming from.

While Zinner transferred money from one trust account to another to give the appearance of solvency, claims began to accumulate; by July 1992, claims were coming at the rate of 1,500 a month. With little available money to pay them, Zinner instructed employees to "whack them"—meaning that very few should receive payment. By August, unpaid claims exceeded $800,000.

By the summer of 1992, Zinner and the Atlantic Plan were under fire from a number of quarters. In June, the Department of Labor began an investigation of the plan. In July, a federal court in California upheld a cease and desist order prohibiting the plan from being sold there, a significant problem given that a third of all Atlantic's premiums were coming from California.

By August, things were so bad that Zinner decided to sell the Atlantic Plan to his former employer, Tony Ullah. Despite Atlantic's large number of unpaid claims, Ullah came out ahead in the deal. In a complicated arrangement, Zinner, in essence, unloaded his problems by paying Ullah to buy the company from him. Ullah was able to then switch policyholders out of the Atlantic Plan and into his own plan, which was still operating legally, under a federal court order, in California. It was a win-win situation. Ullah got many new paying subscribers and Zinner was able to unburden himself of a troubled organization that was under scrutiny by state and federal authorities.

The sale of Atlantic, however, did not mean that Zinner was leaving the MEWA business. Two weeks after the sale, he created the American Plan, which included the American Trust (the actual trust fund) and the American Administrator (the third-party administrator for the trust). Zinner then began marketing the plan nationwide through a network of agents.

Again he misrepresented to the agents the amount of assets held in reserve. He also manipulated the source of insurance for the plan. Zinner told regulators in several states that the American Plan would be fully insured by the Atlantic Fidelity Insurance Company of Arizona, which Zinner had incorporated in January 1993. Zinner's brother was listed as the president of the company and his mother as secretary. The only sign that the company existed anywhere but on paper was an Arizona bank account with $10,000 in it that was closed after a month.

With this shaky financial arrangement in place, Zinner began selling the American Plan in a number of states. Despite the fact that premiums were pouring in, by the end of 1993, the American Plan did not show a profit. The reason was simple. Zinner and his associates were siphoning off the premiums for their own personal use. In February 1994, one of Zinner's chief executives, William Ramsey, who was under the illusion that the plan was legitimate and was operating in the black, learned that the fund was grossly underfunded and that Zinner had removed the initial $250,000 he had put up to start the fund a year earlier. After Ramsey took this information to federal authorities, Zinner fired him. Then, in an attempt to cover up this shortfall of funds, Zinner assigned a promissory note for $124,000 from Equity Development Company, a firm in which he was a partner. The promissory note was worthless.

These cover-up efforts were too little, too late. In January 1995, Zinner, Moulton, and two of Atlantic's employees were charged in a 15-count federal indictment in Philadelphia. Eventually, Zinner was sentenced to serve 68 months in federal prison; his codefendants received sentences of probation and short prison terms.

Zinner's prison sentence put an end not only to his career as an insurance swindler but also to his alter ego, for Edward Zinner was a man who lived two lives. By day he was a wheeling and dealing businessman. By night he was a self-styled rock star who was obsessed with legendary rock figure

Duane Allman, the hard-living guitarist for the Allman Brothers Band who died in a motorcycle accident in the early 1970s. Zinner's own band, Southern Legends, played only Allman Brothers songs, a fact that no doubt limited their appeal and potential success. During the period when he and his associates were ripping off thousands of employees in health insurance scams, Zimmer was pouring thousands of dollars into the band, spending $20,000 for a sound mixing board, $30,000 for a studio, and $65,000 for a tour bus. Despite these investments, the band suffered from a lack of talent and originality and was relegated to the fraternity party circuit at southern colleges.[40]

Zinner did try mixing the people from his two worlds. In 1992, he hired members of his band to answer telephones and do computer work at his insurance operations. When he sought to expand his business ventures by spending insurance funds to build a seafood restaurant (a clam house) in Virginia, he put his band members to work there. The entrepreneurial Zinner also started his own record company, Trashmore Records, Inc., to preserve his band's work for posterity.

Zinner made frequent public statements concerning his views on the small business health insurance industry and insurance regulators. In June 1992, just as his Atlantic Plan was on the verge of collapse and under fire by regulators in numerous states, he appeared before the House Committee on Education and Labor, Subcommittee on Labor-Management Relations in Washington. In his testimony Zinner told the congressional panel:

AHBT [Atlantic Healthcare Benefits Trust] is soundly financed, based on conservative actuarial analysis, and pays benefits regularly and rapidly. . . . We can and do provide a good basic medical benefit plan at less than half the cost of a comprehensive medical insurance policy sponsored by major insurers.[41]

He acknowledged the problems in the MEWA industry but, remarkably, claimed that state regulators were responsible for many of them:

The states are engaging in unscrupulous practices which are blocking access to benefits and often causing unpaid claims situations to occur. That is, MEWAS can be perfectly sound but still be run out of business by certain states.[42]

Later Zinner continued his attacks on state insurance regulators in the press. In a 1993 article, he referred to insurance departments as "the mafia without guns":

State [insurance] departments bark about MEWAS, not because they care about the public but because all they care about is keeping their insurance money and tax money. . . . State governments participate in the lie that people can't afford health care. In the 18 months I've run National Consultants, we've never had one legitimate complaint against us.[43]

Given his affinity for rock music and his tendency towards outrageous public statements, Zinner might appear as an almost sympathetic character, the kind of colorful flim-flam man one finds portrayed in Hollywood movies. This might be the case were it not for his victims, many of whom suffered extreme hardship and suffering as the result of his crimes.

Among those victimized by Zinner and his associates was a Pennsylvania couple whose daughter was born with a serious defect that left her with virtually no skin covering her abdomen. The condition required her to stay in neonatal care for two months while extensive skin graft operations were performed. It also required numerous follow-up operations. During this time, the husband's employer switched health plans to AHBT. The previous insurer had paid for the child's first seven operations, but the parents had to wait as long as 19 months to receive payment. When the child was nearly three years old, an eighth operation was required, the first under the AHBT plan. Eight days before the operation was to be performed, the child's parents called the offices of AHBT to inform them of the impending surgery. A secretary they spoke to told them that their policy did not include coverage of birth defects and congenital diseases and that the plan would not pay the costs of the operation. The parents protested and told the secretary about a letter they had received from the president of AHBT that stated, "your coverage includes full takeover of preexisting conditions." The secretary's response was, "That letter means nothing." [44] The parents were forced to postpone the surgery that would have cost them $20,000 or more while lawyers battled with AHBT over reimbursement.

Another of Zinner's victims, Hank Jaworski,[45] testified at his sentencing hearing. The 49-year-old Jaworski told the court that in 1992 he had dropped his policy with Prudential and enrolled himself, his wife, his daughter, and his son in the Atlantic Healthcare Benefits Trust plan. He had learned of AHBT through the mother of his daughter's friend:

She showed me the policy. It was a nice big piece of literature, they had a booklet, the silver/gray with the maroon lettering on it. And it seemed like a pretty good deal. At the time I had Prudential and their rate was a little bit cheaper than Prudential.[46]

Not long after that, his wife was diagnosed with a rare blood disorder; two months later she died. Treatments for her illness were expensive, eventually totaling between $65,000 and $75,000. As Jaworski explained in court, none of those bills was ever paid:

Nothing was denied, nothing was ever paid. It was never meant to be paid. I can understand that, because, you know, of what's going on here. It's a terrible thing that something like this can happen. And, you know, Mr. Zinner over there dragged a few other people in. I don't know who they are. I have no animosity towards anybody except I'm here because on behalf of my wife who died. I just wanted to come here to see his face so that he could see me and know what pain my family went through.

I have a son and a daughter, they went through it. You know, it hurts when your son comes home from school and says to mommy, mom, did you get any payments yet? Want me to use the phone? I'll dial it for you. And get put on hold and they never pick the phone back up. We'll get back to you. No one is in the accounting department. They probably had no accounting department. And I got phony names like Mrs. York, Mr. DeSpain. You know, it was just a big runaround. It was horrible. It was a horrible thing to experience.[47]

When asked what he planned to do about the bills, Mr. Jaworski replied: "I've been paying. I've been making arrangements with doctors and different people that treated her to make monthly payments on a lower level over a time period."[48]

THE OFFSHORE CONNECTION

As part of their elaborate scheme to defraud employees and employers, Rubell and Helm purchased what is known as *reinsurance* from European insurance companies. Reinsurance is a mechanism by which a *primary insurer*—the insurance company that is underwriting an insurance policy—reduces its risk by ceding part of that risk to another insurer—the *reinsurer*. Typically, reinsurers cover claims above a certain predetermined amount. Reinsurance policies are only valid when the policy from the primary insurer remains in place. When the primary insurer for RHIS terminated its agreement with the MEWA, the European reinsurance policies Rubell-Helm had purchased became worthless. Rubell-Helm's use of European reinsurance was but one example of many in which MEWA scams included offshore insurance companies in their efforts to confuse clients and regulators. To understand the role that these foreign insurers play in MEWA frauds, we need to take a closer look at the murky netherworld of the offshore insurance industry.

In the 1970s and 1980s, offshore insurers assumed prominent roles in the U.S. insurance market. In 1994, a congressional panel reported that "offshore insurers and reinsurers without American operating licenses now hold approximately 40 percent of the commercial market in this country."[49] A significant number of these companies are headquartered in Caribbean countries where regulatory standards are lax and financial secrecy laws make it difficult for U.S. regulators to obtain information. Some of the biggest problems in the off-shore industry have been among Caribbean-based reinsurance companies. In 1990, a congressional panel headed by Representative Dingell that was looking into problems in the insurance industry concluded that the reinsurance industry represented a regulatory "black hole" because of the extremely limited amount of oversight U.S. regulators could extend over companies doing business from offshore.[50]

Dingell's committee was part of a series of congressional hearings held in the early 1990s that turned up evidence of widespread fraud and abuse in the offshore insurance industry. Several of those hearings focused on the exploits of the infamous insurance swindler Alan Teale, who might well be described as the Al Capone of insurance fraud. During the 1980s, British native Teale and his wife, Charlotte Rentz, set up a labyrinth of insurance companies, reinsurers, brokers, and agents that operated within and outside of U.S. borders and ultimately defrauded policyholders out of hundreds of millions of dollars. One colony in Teale's illicit insurance empire was a Pennsylvania-based, licensed insurance company, World Life and Health, which sold insurance policies to MEWAs around the country. A large portion of that insurance was then ceded to reinsurers through a Teale-owned firm, World Re, which placed the insurance with various offshore, unlicensed reinsurers in which Teale and his associates had significant financial interests. Congressional investigators looking into Teale's activities described the relationships among all of these entities in their 1991 report to Congress:

The staff attempted to examine the financial soundness of the reinsurance companies used by World Life and Health. In doing so, the staff confronted what we can only conclude is a regulator's nightmare: a massive web of brokers, financial intermediaries and companies, many of which were located offshore and far beyond the jurisdiction of state regulators. The staff found that the premium income from World Life flowed through this network to fund a host of commissions and fees to these intermediaries, leaving only a few cents on the dollar to protect policyholders. Moreover, the money was channeled to a vast array of accounts, both domestic and foreign, making it nearly impossible for regulators to accurately determine the amount or whereabouts of the funds.[51]

In the end, investigators discovered that Teale's reinsurers collected $7.5 million in premiums from World Life and Health but failed to pay $5.3 million in claims.[52]

World Life, though, was not Teale's only venture into the MEWA industry. During the 1980s Teale was affiliated with an Orlando-based MEWA known as the International Forum of Florida (IFF). In 1983, IFF began selling health insurance to small businesses across the state. Operated as a classic Ponzi scheme, early claims were paid with incoming premiums, but later claims went unpaid as the owners skimmed millions of dollars from the fund. Despite evidence of problems at the company, state insurance regulators were dissuaded from closing IFF down when its operators claimed to have $3 million worth of new assets in reserves. Unfortunately, those assets turned out to be worthless securities provided by Teale. When state regulators finally did shut down IFF in 1990, they found the firm had left some 40,000 policyholders with $29 million in unpaid claims.[53] They also discovered that much of the insurance sold by IFF was placed with Teale-associated offshore reinsurers through World Re, whose president was Teale's wife Charlotte Rentz.[54]

Alan Teale died in 1994 while serving a 17-year sentence in federal prison, but his innovative strategy of combining MEWAS and offshore insurance companies to bilk unsuspecting health insurance policyholders lived on in the scams of other insurance con artists. Another outpost in the far-flung Teale empire was a company called Old American Insurance, domiciled in the Turks and Caicos Islands in the British West Indies. Old American sold insurance to a variety of MEWAS, bogus labor unions (see Chapter 4), and other groups through a cadre of U.S. brokers and agents, whose members included a Colorado businessman named Frank O'Bryan.[55] One of O'Bryan's alleged tasks in the Teale–Old American operations was to set up an "asset renting" scheme in which worthless penny stocks were leased to falsely inflate Old American's assets in an attempt to deceive regulators.[56]

Operating out of offices in Denver, in November 1988, O'Bryan purchased a dormant insurance company that was chartered in the British Virgin Islands; this he promptly renamed Cabot Day Insurance Company. At the same time, O'Bryan, along with business associates in Massachusetts, created a MEWA called Equity Med-Kare, which sold Cabot Day's health insurance to small businesses in at least 15 states.

In its promotional materials, Equity Med-Kare's ERISA status was touted as an advantage for policyholders:

When one adds to the efficiency of an Erisa, the fact is that in the unlikely event of a disputed claim, such a dispute is handled by arbitration through the office of the Department of Labor, thus avoiding the time, expense, and conflicts of state courts, lawyers, state insurance commissions and the attendant delay and complication. It also should be known that it is a federal crime for an Erisa Trust not to pay a ligitimate [*sic*] claim.[57]

In fact, as many of the individuals who signed up with Equity Med-Kare would later discover, the MEWA's purported ERISA status was a major disadvantage for policyholders since the officials at the Department of Labor *did not* have an efficient mechanism in place for handling ERISA plan members' complaints, even assuming that they would have recognized Equity Med-Kare as a bona fide ERISA plan. Moreover, since Equity Med-Kare was not a licensed insurer, when the plan was declared insolvent, policyholders had no possibility of having their unpaid medical claims covered by state guaranty funds as they would have had they been insured by a licensed insurance company.

Prospective clients also were reassured about the strength of the plan's assets:

Although a foreign carrier, Cabot Day maintains its assets and reserves within the United States, making them available within this country, should the need arise. The amount of reserves maintained by Cabot Day is kept at a level at least equal to the requirements of the most stringent state regulatory authorities. As of December 31, 1988, Cabot Day held assets in excess of $10,000,000, and the asset base has steadily increased over the course of the year.[58]

Contrary to this statement, federal prosecutors would later assert that "In fact, Cabot Day had virtually no assets."[59]

Despite the fractured grammar and spelling errors in its promotional material, Equity Med-Kare was enormously successful in signing up clients. According to federal prosecutors, in the course of one year, Cabot Day and Equity Med-Kare took in $5.72 million in health insurance premiums while paying out only $894,940 in claims. When the operation shut down in 1990, policyholders were left with $5.74 million in unpaid claims.[60]

Among Equity Med-Kare's numerous victims was Don Collins, a 51-year-old auto mechanic in Forth Worth, Texas. After his wife's employer, a small optical service company, switched to Equity Med-Kare's plan in 1989, Mrs. Collins suffered a recurrence of cancer, for which she had first been treated the previous year. By January 1990, when Texas regulators shut Equity Med-Kare down, Mrs. Collins's medical bills totaled more than $30,000; her insurer refused to pay any portion. Thereafter, Mrs. Collins had no health insurance, and in July of that year when she passed away, her husband was left with medical debts of over $100,000.[61]

Equity Med-Kare's victims also included the employees of a small school district in Hidalgo County, Texas. The district's business manager had purchased a group policy with the Denver-based MEWA in September 1989 after the organization submitted a bid that was $20 per employee, per month lower than other bidders—an annual savings to the district of $60,000. During the last quarter of 1989, the school district paid Equity Med-Kare over $64,000 in premiums and submitted $50,000 in claims, including $40,000 for an employee who had suffered a stroke. None of these claims was ever paid.[62]

In February 1992, O'Bryan and four associates were indicted by a federal grand jury in Philadelphia, and the next year all pleaded guilty to charges connected to the fraudulent Equity Med-Kare and Cabot Day. O'Bryan could have been sentenced to a prison term of over fifteen years, but his sentence was suspended on the condition that he provide federal authorities with information on other insurance swindles.[63]

As evidence that you can't keep a good white-collar criminal down, in 1994, O'Bryan established a new company, Progressive Administrators Inc. (PAI), which purportedly sold medical storage units. O'Bryan's partner in this venture was none other than his official "handler"—an assistant U.S. Attorney who had been assigned to work with the consummate con artist to develop information about other insurance scams. In 1996, local and federal authorities began investigating PAI on suspicions that the firm had swindled investors out of $243,000. When federal prosecutors back in Philadelphia heard about the investigation, they immediately moved to have O'Bryan's suspended sentenced reinstated. He was soon ordered to spend six and a half years in prison.[64] In June 1997, O'Bryan's partner, the former federal prosecutor, pleaded guilty to charges involving bribery and investment fraud.[65]

Unlicensed insurance companies operating outside the borders of the United States figured prominently in many of the health insurance scams examined for this study. In this list of offshore insurers, the same names cropped up over and over as the purported providers of insurance coverage to small employers in the United States, many of whom were unaware of the companies' existence. The fact that these foreign entities are generally unregulated by and unaccountable to American authorities is a great advantage for health insurance crooks. When the onshore operators of bogus MEWAs or unions are forced to admit that they are incapable of paying off claims, they frequently declare that they too had been victimized by these unscrupulous and often unseen foreign entities, conveniently forgetting to mention their own close ties to these supposedly distant companies. Regulators are thus left in a quandary trying to connect the dots in a puzzle of interconnected brokers, ERISA plans, onshore and offshore insurance companies, and their often dubious assets. By the time they have finally made all these connections, the crooks have bilked their clients out of millions of dollars, proving the old adage that the devil is indeed in the details.

CONCLUSIONS

The idea behind MEWAs is a good one. They represent a means by which small employers can enjoy the same economies of scale as do large corporations to provide their employees with health care, workers' compensation, and other benefits. ERISA gave these pools or trusts a competitive edge over commercial insurers by exempting them from the administrative burden of state regulation and the higher costs it imposes. But this strength is also a serious weakness. The absence of rigorous state or federal regulation has been a open invitation to con artists who see tremendous potential for illicit profit in MEWAs. Michael Rubell, James Helm, and Edward Zinner were but a few of the many people who have created MEWAs, taken in millions of dollars in premiums, diverted hundreds of thousands of dollars for their own personal use, and left thousands of individuals with unpaid medical claims.

The possibilities for MEWA fraud are greatly enhanced by the complicated nature of the health insurance industry itself. From the consumer's point of view, even legitimate health insurance plans often appear to be a confusing tangle of interconnected organizations and arcane terminology: *primary insurer, reinsurer, stop-loss insurance,* and so on. Consumers are left with little basis for discriminating between legitimate and illegitimate health plans, and because until recently MEWAs were generally unlicensed by states, consumers have not been able to call the state insurance department to verify MEWA promoters' claims. Under these conditions, simple things like "official looking" promotional literature may convince people like Hank Jaworski to sign up with a health plan. Consumers may also be unaware of the distinction between a licensed and unlicensed insurer, and claims such as those made by the operators of Equity Med-Kare that the federal oversight of their ERISA plan was actually superior to the state regulation imposed on traditional insurance companies may seem persuasive.

Following the MEWA scandals of the late 1980s and early 1990s, many states passed legislation that placed MEWAS under state regulatory authority and required MEWA owners to obtain licenses before they started signing up clients. These new laws did indeed make it more difficult for the Michael Rubells and Edward Zinners of the world to use MEWAS as their own personal piggy banks. By the mid-1990s, law enforcement officials were no longer seeing the large-scale, multistate MEWA scams that flourished in the 1980s. Instead, health insurance scam artists were using different organizational vehicles to perpetrate their crimes.

In the fall of 1993, the Office of the Inspector General, U.S. Department of Labor commented on this shift in strategy in the office's semiannual report:

Some operators fleeing the enhanced scrutiny given MEWAs have turned to bogus unions for refuge. OLR [Office of Labor Racketeering] investigations have revealed that these "unions" are in fact, fraudulent and/or bogus unions. Consequently, OLR has shifted its focus from MEWA fraud to the increasing number of health insurance schemes that are being marketed as if they were sponsored by labor unions.[66]

This decline in MEWA fraud was actually in the number of health insurance organizations that *claimed* to be MEWAS. As Chapters 3 and 4 discuss, in many cases involving employee leasing firms and bogus unions, federal authorities would claim that the organizations were in fact MEWAS and therefore subject to limited state regulation, an argument that the plans' operators would strenuously deny. Nonetheless, the increased attention given by the Department of Labor and state regulators

to MEWA operators and the enactment of regulatory laws in
many states did result in a decline in the number of organizations that hid behind ERISA's MEWA provisions when stealing
health insurance premiums from employees.

NOTES

1 John Emshwiller, "'Unscrupulous Promoters' of MEWAs Cause Problems
for Small Businesses," *Wall Street Journal*, 15 May 1990, p. B2.

2 Senate Committee on Governmental Affairs, Permanent Subcommittee
on Investigations, *Interim Report on Combating Fraud and Abuse in
Employer Sponsored Health Benefit Plans*, 102d Cong., 2d sess., 12 May
1992, 17–18.

3 Greg David, "Employer Benefit Trusts' Growth Alarms Officials; More
Failures Feared," *Business Insurance*, 21 February 1977, p. 1.

4 Franklin Damon, "Multiple Employer Trusts—A Historical Perspective
from ERISA to the California Approach," *Journal of Insurance Regulation* 2 (1983): 20–29.

5 Jerry Giesel, "California Probing Why Giant MET Ran Out of Funds,"
Business Insurance, 4 October 1982, p. 1.

6 Eric Miller, "Insurance Trust for Ministers Draws State Investigation,"
Dallas Morning News, 19 July 1981, p. 1A.

7 Todd Vogel, "6 Health Firms Closed," *Dallas Morning News*, 18 September 1985, p. 21A; Senate Committee on Governmental Affairs, Permanent Subcommittee on Investigations, *Fraud and Abuse in Employer
Sponsored Health Benefit Plans*, 101st Cong., 2d sess., 15 May 1990,
124.

8 Senate Committee, *Interim Report*, 4.

9 *United States v. Helm*, No. 93-545 (A)-MRP (C. D. Cal. 1993) (docs.).

10 Ibid.

11 Ibid.

12 Senate Committee, *Fraud and Abuse in Employer Sponsored Health
Benefit Plans*, 140.

13 Ibid., statement of Jo Ann Howard, Texas State Board of Insurance, attachment C.

14 *United States v. Helm*, note 9 *supra*, documents.

15 Department of Labor, Office of the Inspector General, "Former California Health Insurance Executive Pleads Guilty in Extensive Group Health and Life Insurance Scam," press release, 31 March 1992.

16 Department of Labor, Office of the Inspector General, "Former California Health Insurance Executive Pleads Guilty in Group Health, Life Insurance Scam," press release, 31 August 1991.

17 Ibid.

18 *United States v. Helm,* note 9 *supra,* documents.

19 Ibid.

20 Ibid.

21 Ibid.

22 House Select Committee on Aging, Subcommittee on Retirement Income and Employment, *Small Business and Older Workers Health Benefits: Multiple Employer Welfare Arrangements, The Problem or the Solution?* 102d Cong., 1st sess., 17 September 1991, 218–20.

23 Janet Robinson is a pseudonym.

24 *United States v. Helm,* note 9 *supra,* documents.

25 Janet Parker is a pseudonym.

26 *United States v. Helm,* note 9 *supra,* documents.

27 Senate Committee, *Fraud and Abuse in Employer Sponsored Health Benefit Plans,* 140.

28 "California Says Firm Didn't Place Insurance for Employee Groups," *Wall Street Journal,* 10 March 1989, p. B2.

29 Senate Committee, *Fraud and Abuse in Employer Sponsored Health Benefit Plans,* statement of Jo Ann Howard, attachment C.

30 Senate Committee, *Fraud and Abuse in Employer Sponsored Health Benefit Plans.*

31 Ibid., 13.

32 Senate Committee, *Interim Report,* 9.

33 Douglas McLeod, "MEWA Fight Bedevils Regulators," *Business Insurance,* 17 April 1995, p. 1.

34 *IAEA v. Missouri,* 58 F.3d 1266 (8th Cir. 1995).

35 Much of the following discussion is taken from court documents related to *United States v. Zinner,* No. 95–48 (E.D. Pa. 1995). Particularly useful was the presentence investigation report for Jeffry Neal.

36 The United Healthcare Association was in no way connected to the health maintenance organization, United HealthCare.

37 *United States v. Zinner,* note 35 *supra,* presentence investigation report, Jeffry Neal, p. 9.

38 U.S. Department of Labor, Pension and Welfare Benefits Administration, Opinion 92-32, 1991.

39 *AHBT v. Goggins,* 2 F.3d 1 (2d Cir. 1993).

40 Marc Davis, "A Double Life, and Then a Fall," *Virginia Pilot,* 11 November 1995, p. 29A.

41 House Committee on Education and Labor, Subcommittee on Labor-Management Relations, *Hearing on H.R. 2773, H.R. 4919, and H.R. 5386,* 102d Cong., 2d sess., 16 June 1992, 215–16.

42 Ibid., 220.

43 Tom Johnson, "Health Insurance Con Artists Prey on Small Businesses as Health Costs Rise," *Warfields Business Record,* 2 July 1993, p. 7.

44 Senate Committee on Labor and Human Resources, testimony of Josephine Musser, National Association of Insurance Commissioners, 15 March 1995.

45 Hank Jaworski is a pseudonym.

46 *United States v. Zinner,* note 35 *supra,* sentencing transcript.

47 Ibid.

48 Ibid.

49 House Committee on Energy and Commerce, Subcommittee on Oversight and Investigations, *Wishful Thinking: A World View of Insurance Solvency Regulation,* 103d Cong., 2d sess., October 1994, 3.

50 House Committee on Energy and Commerce, Subcommittee on Oversight and Investigations, *Failed Promises: Insurance Company Insolvencies.* 101st Cong., 2d sess., February 1990, 60–61.

51 Senate Committee on Governmental Affairs, Permanent Subcommittee on Investigations, *Efforts to Combat Fraud and Abuse in the Insurance Industry,* pt. II, 102d Cong., 2d sess., 26 June 1991, 80.

52 Douglas McLeod, "6 Charged in Scam with Teale," *Business Insurance,* 12 February 1996, p. 3.

53 Creston Nelson-Merrill, "Fla. MEWA Fraud Left 40,000 Bare," *National Underwriter,* 18 January 1993, p. 4.

54 Senate Committee, *Efforts to Combat Fraud and Abuse,* testimony of Tom Gallagher, Florida Insurance Commissioner, 165.

55 *Bailey v. Empire Blue Cross/Blue Shield,* No. 93-CV-6179 (S.D.N.Y. 1993) ("Third Amended Complaint").

56 Douglas McLeod, "New Complaint Filed in Fraud Suit," *Business Insurance,* 4 March 1996, p. 53.

57 Senate Committee, *Fraud and Abuse in Employer Sponsored Health Benefit Plans,* statement of Jo Ann Howard, attachment B.

58 Ibid.

59 U.S. Attorney's Office, Eastern District of Pennsylvania, press release, 3 February 1992.

60 Ibid.

61 Bill Lodge, "Premium of Pain," *Dallas Morning News,* 4 November 1990, p. 22.

62 Ibid.

63 *United States v. O'Bryan,* No. 92-CR-27-02 (E.D. Pa. 1992) ("Government's Sentencing Memorandum").

64 Howard Pankratz, "Fraud Probe Targets Con Artist, Federal 'Handler'," *Denver Post,* 20 October 1996, p. A-1.

65 Howard Pankratz, "Ex-Prosecutor Pleads Guilty to Taking Gifts," *Denver Post,* 19 June 1997, p. B-3.

66 U.S. Department of Labor, Office of Inspector General, *Semiannual Report to the Congress, April 1–September 30, 1993* (Washington, D.C.: GPO, 1993), 42.

Employee Leasing Scams

I N the 1980s, as small businesses faced increased competition, many discovered that it was more economical to turn over personnel functions—payroll, pension plan management, and the administration of health care benefits—to outside firms. Thus, a new industry emerged: *employee leasing*. Under these arrangements, employers "fire" their employees who are then "hired" (at least on paper) by leasing firms who are responsible for managing payroll and benefits. In many cases, the change is transparent to employees who continue to work for the same employers under the same conditions as before. The arrangement is particularly attractive to small business owners who are no longer saddled with the responsibility of administering employee benefits. Moreover, by banding together with other small employers they can take advantage of economies of scale that allow them to purchase health insurance at reduced rates.

The idea of employee leasing caught on quickly. In 1984, there were an estimated 98 leasing firms in operation, employing about 10,000 workers. By 1993, there were over 2,100 leasing firms doing business across the country, offering benefits and providing payroll services for 1.6 million employees.[1] The number of leased workers increased to 2.5 million by

1995, and those numbers were predicted to rise dramatically in the future.[2]

Despite its advantages, there is clearly a downside to employee leasing. Employers no longer have control over such critical benefits as medical and pension plans. Leasing firms, sometimes very "fly by night" operations, assume responsibility for these crucial areas, which significantly impact the lives of workers and their families. In addition, leasing firms take over responsibility for providing workers' compensation, which opens up the possibility of stealing from those funds.

CAP STAFFING

Regulators, law enforcement agents, and lawmakers received a wake-up call in 1989 when the employee leasing firm Cap Staffing collapsed, leaving 1,350 policyholders with $2 million in unpaid claims. The events surrounding Cap Staffing's demise revealed how, in a very short period of time, large amounts of money could be lost and large numbers of people victimized in employee leasing scams.

Cap Staffing was created in the summer of 1988 in Charlotte, North Carolina, by Robert Long, whose previous work experience consisted of leasing dental equipment, and Ron Harris, who claimed to be a former insurance executive. In the fall of 1988, Cap Staffing signed an agreement with Travelers Insurance of Connecticut under which Travelers would serve as a third-party administrator—processing claims and performing other administrative duties—for the health plan Cap Staffing was offering to its leased employees. Under the agreement, Travelers did not underwrite the insurance. Instead, the plan was to be self-funded, meaning that all claims had to be paid from the premiums sent in by clients.

Over the next six months Cap Staffing's sales agents signed up dozens of employers into the health plan by telling them that it was fully insured by Travelers. The strategy was an enormous success. By May 1989, Cap Staffing was insur-

ing over 3,000 employees who were collectively sending in
$275,000 in monthly premiums.

In early June 1989, Long and Harris sold Cap Staffing to a
firm called GEMCO, a Florida company whose primary business involved gold mining in Nevada. GEMCO was run by two
partners, Michael Spieles and Michael Krebser. Under the
terms of the sales agreement, Long and Harris continued to
manage the daily operations of the employee leasing firm,
which was renamed Universal Staffing Associates.

According to Travelers, "between June 2, and July 31,
1989, while GEMCO purportedly owned Cap Staffing, Spieles
and Krebser apparently siphoned off in excess of $1 million
from Cap Staffing."[3] On August 1, 1989, Travelers terminated
its relationship with Cap/Universal. The Connecticut insurance company ended up paying nearly $900,000 in medical
claims that the leasing company should have paid.[4]

The withdrawal of Travelers was the beginning of the end
for Cap Staffing. In March 1990, the company sent out letters
to all policyholders informing them that the firm was "technically insolvent." Even then, the company's owners attempted
to bilk their customers out of more money, informing them
that only the holders of policies that were fully paid would
have their medical claims covered and therefore anyone with
a delinquent account should send in what they owed if they
wanted to receive claim monies.[5]

Cap Staffing and the misdeeds of its owners were the focus
of congressional hearings in May 1990, headed by Sen. Sam
Nunn. At those hearings the pain and suffering endured by the
victims of the fraudulent leasing firm were detailed. Many of
those victimized were low wage workers who lived at the edge
of a marginal material existence. For many, their experiences
with Cap Staffing pushed them over that edge. This was the
case with Carolyn Sharpe, who described her situation in a
letter to Senator Nunn. In her letter Sharpe explained that she
had taken a job at a Taco Bell in Lugoff, South Carolina, to
obtain health insurance for herself and three children. She was
told initially that the insurance was from Travelers but later

learned it was being provided by Cap Staffing. In August 1989, Sharpe was told by her physician that she had cervical cancer and would have to have a hysterectomy. A few days later, Sharpe and her coworkers at Taco Bell were informed that their health insurance policy had been canceled. In her letter (reproduced here as originally written), she described what happened next:

Because I had no insurance the nurse at Dr. Beacon's office told me I'd have to get some financial help before they'd schedule my surgery. They sent me to a social worker, but she said we made to much money.

We went through pure hell for nearly four months trying to figure out a way to get my surgery done. Not knowing if the waiting was killing me.

We'd done everything we could think of, my husband went to several insurance companies trying to get insurance on me. They told him they didn't know anyone that would insure me with prediagnosed cancer. Then he went job hunting; he went to five different places. One of them said their insurance would cover me so he took an unsafe job so I could have my surgery. The insurance cost $44.00 a week and was $300.00 deductible. I didn't trust them so I checked with them myself. They told me because I had been prediagnosed they would just pay $5,000.00 on my surgery.

I thought my troubles was over they scheduled my surgery. About a week before I was to go in the hospital, the people at the hospital started calling me wanting to know who was gona pay the rest of my bill. I tried to explain to them that I was trying to sue the insurance company for the money. Every day they were calling me at work telling me I had to get my employer to say he'd pay the rest of my bill or I'd have to pay the difference before I went in the hospital. My lawyer . . . called them and must have straightened them out. I went in and had my surgery; scared to death, I didn't know what to expect next.

I hope these people are caught and put away for life. I'm just one of many they've done like this. I can't began to tell you the stress and pain my family has went through because of this.

When Cap Staffing's original owner, Robert Long, appeared before Senator Nunn's committee in May 1990, the

senator asked him how he felt about what had happened to
people like Sharpe. He replied:

My whole insides are eaten out and I would just love to be able to
help them. My insides have been eaten out, like I said, for a year
now, since this happened, and I have been through a severe depression because of it.[7]

Long's depression, however, was apparently not too severe to
prevent him from starting a new employee leasing firm after
he left Cap Staffing. Nor was it too severe to have prevented
him from taking a Caribbean cruise in 1989, one of the purposes of which, Senator Nunn hinted, may have been to set up
offshore bank accounts to launder money from Cap Staffing.[8]

Just eight months later, in December 1990, Long, Harris,
Spieles, Krebser, and two other men were indicted in a federal
court in North Carolina. All would eventually plead guilty and
be sentenced to prison terms ranging from two to six years.[9]

IN THE LATE 1980s and early 1990s, dozens of questionable
if not outright fraudulent employee leasing firms cropped up
around the country. Many of them did business in Sun Belt
states such as Florida and Texas. By 1991, Texas Attorney
General Dan Morales was characterizing the state's employee
leasing industry as "fraught with unscrupulous con artists."[10]
One of the firms to which Morales was referring was known
as American Workforce, whose head was a corpulent, middle-
aged entrepreneur named James Borgelt.

AMERICAN WORKFORCE [11]

In the early 1980s, Borgelt owned several Dallas-area employee leasing firms: Omnistaff, Unistaff, and Ultrastaff. When
all three firms filed for bankruptcy in 1985, allegations of
fraud surfaced, but no criminal charges were filed. Eventually,
the Internal Revenue Service (IRS) assessed penalties totaling

$7 million against Borgelt for failure to pay withheld payroll taxes from leased employees.

Apparently undeterred by this financial setback, Borgelt returned to the employee leasing industry in 1988, when he became the de facto head of a new firm, American Workforce (AWF). AWF emerged when Miller Personnel Inc., a small Texas temporary employee firm, was purchased out of bankruptcy proceedings by Staffing Systems, Inc., which ostensibly was owned by Ernesto Ornelas, but in fact was controlled by Borgelt. Although he had no formal title at Staffing Systems, he maintained control of the firm by obtaining an option to acquire 80 percent of its stock. All of this took place while, in an effort to avoid his IRS liability, Borgelt filed for personal bankruptcy. Later, he would further disguise his involvement in AWF by obtaining an option and proxy for 60 percent of the shares in the firm issued to his son, James Borgelt Jr. Borgelt Sr. filed documents with the Department of Labor claiming that AWF was a single employer offering an employee benefit plan and was therefore subject to ERISA and not to state insurance regulations.

With Borgelt at the helm, AWF experienced spectacular growth, aggressively marketing its services in several states through a company known as B&M International Marketing, 90 percent of which was owned by Borgelt. In 1989, AWF reported only 500 leased employees. By late 1990, it reported 7,000. By the final quarter of 1990, AWF paid wages of $23 million to Texas employees alone. At the peak of its short life, AWF was one of the largest employee leasing firms in the country.

This dramatic growth hid the fact that AWF was deeply insolvent. In 1990, the firm lost $7.1 million on gross revenues of approximately $103 million. These losses were the inevitable consequence of the fact that AWF's services were underpriced and its plans could not possibly operate on a financially sound basis. In addition, Borgelt and his associates were siphoning off large portions of their clients' payments in the form of hefty commissions and salaries. As in other forms of financial frauds in other industries, asset growth and fraud were intimately linked in the case of AWF.[12]

While AWF sank deeper in debt, Borgelt and his family prospered. As a leased employee himself, Borgelt was paid an annual salary of over $200,000. Approximately $450,000 of AWF's funds were used to purchase a house for Borgelt. His son was paid $160,000 a year, and other family members were placed on the payroll of AWF and its affiliated companies and paid large salaries, even though they apparently did very little actual work.

The AWF scandal involved several schemes, but the one that generated the most money was the medical plan that AWF offered to employers. One of the reasons the organization was so successful in signing up employer clients was because the clients believed that the health plan offered by AWF was fully insured by large, reputable insurance companies, one of which was Hartford Life. AWF's agents used its connection with Hartford to tell prospective clients that the insurance giant fully insured the AWF health plan, when, in fact, Hartford only administered the plan—a critical difference.

Employers who signed leasing contracts sent a check to AWF every month equal to the amount of their payroll plus 20 to 30 percent to cover benefits and AWF's administrative costs and profit. These monies were to be placed into different funds, or trusts, to pay for medical benefits, a pension plan, and workers' compensation premiums. However, AWF insiders did not allocate appropriate levels of funding to the medical plan, but instead diverted funds into other employee plans and siphoned off many dollars for their personal use. Even had they put the designated funds into the appropriate account, the health plan would have been grossly underfunded. The $38 per employee per month earmarked for the health insurance fund was nowhere near adequate to provide medical benefits. In other words, the health plan was simply a Ponzi scheme that could not have possibly succeeded. By the fourth quarter of 1990, when the cash flow declined, AWF began to "slow pay" claims, delaying payment for as long as possible, and then ceased payments on health claims altogether.

AWF's motto, "We change people's lives," turned out to be all too true. In addition to those individuals who were left by AWF with unpaid medical claims—some totaling more than $100,000—a number of former AWF "employees" were left unable to obtain health coverage after AWF went into bankruptcy, because of preexisting conditions. One woman who worked for a small fan distributor in Dallas was forced to borrow $5,000 to pay for a hysterectomy after her post-AWF "employer" (another leasing firm) alleged that she failed to disclose the condition on her application to the plan.[13]

The underfunded health care plan was but one of several fraudulent schemes operated from under the AWF umbrella. AWF also gave leased employees the option of contributing 3 percent of their paychecks to a 401(k) pension plan, which the leasing firm claimed it would match with an equal contribution. Employees' contributions were placed in a trust overseen by trustees that included longtime associates of Borgelt, all of whom took their directions from Borgelt. The 401(k) plan, whose titular head was Don Diaz, Borgelt's personal chauffeur, became another cash cow for Borgelt and his associates; no matching contributions were ever made.

Rather than simply pocketing the 401(k) contributions, AWF insiders devised a scheme that allowed them to generate sizeable cash payments to themselves. All employees who elected to participate in the 401(k) plan were required to purchase life insurance policies, which later turned out to be virtually worthless. Insurance brokers who obtained the policies from licensed insurers were paid generous commissions by the carriers, which they then split with Borgelt. Investigators later estimated that during AWF's short life span, Borgelt received some $600,000 via this illegal, fee-splitting mechanism. In the end, AWF employees lost approximately $1 million to the pension fund scheme.

In a separate scheme, AWF defrauded the state of Texas's workers' compensation program of $2.9 million by misclassifying job codes of its leased employees and not reporting pay-roll. The premiums that companies pay to obtain workers' compensation insurance for their employees are based on job classification codes that add to a base premium a *modifier*—a multiplier that is determined by how hazardous their jobs are and by the average number and size of claims within the firm's industry. By reclassifying roofers as, say, clerical workers, a midsized construction company could save thousands of dollars a year in premium payments. This kind of misclassification and underreporting of employees on their payrolls was at the heart of AWF's rip-off of the workers' compensation program.

On March 6, 1991, less than three years after it started up, American Workforce filed for Chapter 11 bankruptcy. Claims against AWF and related entities totaled $27 million, of which $3.5 million consisted of unpaid medical claims. Two years later, in March 1993, the state of Texas and trustees of the leasing firm filed suit against Borgelt, AWF insiders, and associated companies for violation of the conditions of the bankruptcy.

On December 6, 1995, James Borgelt Sr. was indicted by the U.S. Attorney's Office in the Northern District of Texas on various federal charges, including embezzlement from an ERISA plan. In June 1996, Borgelt entered a guilty plea to a single count. As part of a plea agreement, he was sentenced to serve 36 months in prison, despite the fact that federal sentencing guidelines called for a period of imprisonment of 63 to 78 months. In agreeing to a downward departure from the guidelines, federal prosecutors cited the facts that the 64-year-old Borgelt was (at 400 pounds) "grossly overweight" and suffered from a serious medical condition that caused him to stop breathing while asleep and argued that "Mr. Borgelt's overall health is so poor that his life expectancy is extremely short."

One of the more interesting aspects of the AWF case is the extent to which legitimate financial institutions contributed to the fraudulent schemes. In order to assure clients that their funds were being handled properly, Borgelt set up a trust account, into which all clients' contributions were placed, with the Bank of America (BofA), named as the trustee. Part of the agreement between AWF and Bank of America required that BA Davenport, an affiliate of BofA, generate regular reports on the amounts of money to be transferred to the various accounts in the trust. Two years after AWF filed for bankruptcy, the attorney general of Texas filed a civil suit against Bank of America and its affiliates for failing their fiduciary responsibilities in overseeing the trust. Specifically, the suit claimed that "rather than functioning as independent checks on, *inter alia,* the receipt and application of fiduciary funds, Bank of America and BA Davenport ignored their respective fiduciary duties and allowed their conduct to be directed by others under the control of Borgelt, Sr. and those acting in concert with him, perpetuating the false illusion that monies were safe." [14] In the suit, the Texas attorney general and the Texas Department of Insurance alleged that BofA either knew or should have known about the inconsistencies in the AWF trust.

Hartford Life and Accident Insurance Company was also named as a defendant in the civil suit. Texas officials pointed to a letter by a Hartford agent explicitly authorizing AWF to represent to prospective clients that it was fully insured by Hartford as evidence of the insurer's willing involvement in the scheme. According to the lawsuit, "Hartford itself induced and aided and abetted such representations although it knew or should have known that such 'insurance' either did not exist or lacked the advertised and represented characteristics. Hartford also knew that the amounts of employee contributions to medical benefits were grossly inadequate to cover claims." [15] The suit also alleged that Hartford knew that Borgelt was in charge of AWF and was well aware of his difficulties with the IRS.

Hartford denied the allegations, arguing that they too were victims of the AWF scheme. Despite these claims, in the spring of 1994, Hartford settled the suit by agreeing to pay more than $4 million to cover the costs of claims filed by AWF em-

ployees between January and March 1991.[16] The Hartford
settlement was only one of several that the state of Texas negotiated with several large firms that had been associated with
AWF. In 1992, Great West Life Insurance Company agreed to
pay $1.6 million in health insurance claims and $3.2 million
into the Miller Personnel bankruptcy estate to cover other
debts.[17] In that same year, National Western Life Insurance
Company of Colorado agreed to pay approximately $2.5 mil-
lion to cover unpaid 401(k) plan contributions.[18] The state
also obtained $1 million in a settlement with a Dallas law firm
that represented AWF insiders in the bankruptcy case, after officials claimed that a principal at the firm was responsible for
allowing $3 million to be diverted from the estate.[19]

The notoriety that he achieved during the early 1990s was
not the first time that Borgelt had received media attention. In
1984, the *New York Times* ran several stories on the newly
emerging employee leasing industry, one of which featured
Borgelt, who was then running Omnistaff in Dallas. The article was a generally positive portrayal of a man who was on
the cutting edge of a new workplace concept.[20] In that same
year, a feature article on Borgelt appeared in the *Dallas Morning News* in which he was quoted as saying, "employee leasing is a deal where everybody wins. It's a concept whose time
has come."[21]

In 1990, Borgelt was featured in an article that appeared in
a Tulsa, Oklahoma, newspaper. Citing the recent failure of
Oklahoma-based Alliance Temporary Services amidst allegations of fraud (see Chapter 4), the article noted that AWF was
"avoiding the pitfalls" of other firms by doing things like establishing a trust account at Bank of America. Moreover, to
spread the word on successful tactics in the industry, Borgelt
was giving money to Oklahoma City University to set up an
"Institute for the Study of Alternative Staffing Strategies" that
would conduct classes on how to set up and operate leasing
firms.[22] Apparently, neither the author of the article nor officials at the university were aware of the facts that Borgelt had
only five years earlier run three leasing firms into the ground

and owed the IRS $7 million. Nor could they have been aware that in only a year and a half his AWF would file for Chapter 11 and soon thereafter he and his associates would be charged with numerous civil and criminal violations.

RECYCLING INSURANCE FRAUD

In most states employee leasing companies are not required to obtain licenses, nor are their owners and operators required to undergo background checks before their firms start signing up clients. The simple precaution of disqualifying persons from working in the industry who have prior criminal convictions or who have had regulatory sanctions imposed on them could have prevented a number of illegal leasing company operators from fleecing employees out of millions of dollars. What one sees again and again is a pattern in which employee leasing scam artists, after ripping off clients and being shut down by state regulators, simply move to another state where they create new companies under new names and start the cycle all over. In some instances, they don't even bother to leave the state but simply create new companies in the name of "straw owners" and continue with business as usual, often with the same clients from the old company. This pattern was in evidence in the wake of the AWF collapse, as many agents and brokers who once worked for Borgelt went out and started their own employee leasing companies, in some cases targeting the same clients who had just been ripped off by AWF.

In the late 1980s, Texas had no law that prohibited individuals with prior criminal records from working in the employee leasing industry. This fact allowed people like Robert "Skip" Anderson to go to work for AWF, despite the fact that in 1989 he had served six months of a two-year prison sentence in California for bankruptcy fraud. Had regulators been able to check his background they might also have discovered that just prior to moving to Texas, Anderson had been involved with an employee leasing firm in southern California known as U.M.C., Inc., along with a partner, John Junk, who had a long history in the labor leasing business. U.M.C. was just one of a series of leasing companies set up by Junk and several associates during the late 1980s that ripped off both employer-clients and the state by misrepresenting the number of their employees and their job classifications.[23] In November 1989, Anderson applied to the state for workers' compensation insurance claiming that U.M.C. had an annual payroll of $500,000. In fact, U.M.C.'s annual payroll obligations exceeded $20 million. The state issued a policy to U.M.C. on November 8, 1989, but canceled the policy two months later when it discovered the connection between U.M.C. and its predecessors.[24]

Not only was Anderson involved in crooked labor leasing firms before he joined AWF but immediately after he left the company as well. Along with several other AWF alumni, Anderson started Prime Compensation, a Dallas-based leasing firm. One of the companies they targeted was a Dallas graphics firm, whose owner, after losing money to AWF, was approached by representatives of Prime who claimed they had learned their lesson from AWF and were ready to "do things better." Unfortunately for its employees, the graphics firm's owner signed up with Prime and the workers again lost money in unpaid pension benefits and medical claims when Prime went bankrupt.[25]

In 1992, soon after the collapse of Prime, Anderson returned to California where he cofounded a new employee leasing firm, Hazar, Inc. Despite his checkered background, Anderson, along with his partners, was able to quickly build Hazar into what company officials claimed was the largest employee leasing firm in the country. Much of this growth was accomplished through a strategy of buying up smaller leasing firms. By 1994, the company had 24 subsidiaries serving 1,700 client companies with a total of 30,000 employees. In 1993, the company claimed to have revenues of $350 million.[26]

Hazar's fortunes began to fade in February 1994 when its San Francisco offices were raided by agents from the Federal

Bureau of Investigation (FBI) and the Department of Labor, both of whom were investigating allegations that, through its subsidiaries, Hazar had diverted health insurance premiums from leased employees.[27] In April 1994, Hazar filed for Chapter 11 bankruptcy with debts of $30.4 million and assets of only $14.1 million.[28] Hazar executives blamed many of the company's problems on its former controlling shareholder, Skip Anderson. In a civil suit, Hazar claimed that Anderson and his associates had systematically looted the company. The specific charges included:

- putting Anderson's wife on Hazar's payroll at an annual salary of $120,000, which was later increased to $300,000;

- giving Anderson's son a $32,000-a-year job at the company, for which he did virtually no work;

- using $225,000 of Hazar's funds to pay off Anderson's personal legal debts;

- causing Hazar to be liable for $500,000 in debts from Anderson's previous ventures at Prime Compensation and other businesses.[29]

In 1996, seven years after he was released from a California prison, Anderson was convicted in federal court on charges related to his activities at the southern California leasing firm, U.M.C., and was sentenced to serve 27 months in prison and pay $300,000 in restitution.[30] His strange career in the employee leasing industry well illustrates how gaping loopholes in state regulations have allowed known conmen to move from state to state setting up fraudulent leasing firms with little or no capital investment, run those firms as Ponzi schemes, and depart a year or two later with hundreds of thousands of dollars of their leased employees' money.

But Skip Anderson was not the only AWF veteran who decided to make a career out of employee leasing theft. Indeed, in retrospect it appears that AWF was a veritable academy in the fine arts of fraud and deceit in the labor leasing industry. Consider another AWF alumnus, Jerry Burnett.[31]

In 1983, Burnett was charged by Utah prosecutors with eight felony counts of theft in a case involving pension fund assets. He was eventually convicted in the case, but the conviction was later overturned by an appellate court on a technicality. This brush with the law, however, did not prevent Burnett from finding employment several years later with AWF in Dallas. In April 1991, when AWF declared bankruptcy, Burnett took several of his former employer's clients and opened his own leasing company, Employment Resource Services (ERS); six months later he started a second leasing firm, National Staff Alliance (NSA). In 1992, after Texas enacted a law requiring that all employee leasing firms obtain licenses from the state (which meant they had to meet certain financial requirements), Burnett moved the companies to Colorado, which had no licensing law. According to federal investigators, after being in business for two and a half years, the two companies and Burnett owed the Internal Revenue Service and state tax agencies over $1 million in unpaid taxes. In January 1994, when their liabilities grossly outweighed their assets, Burnett did what his mentor James Borgelt had done under similar circumstances. He put the two companies into bankruptcy.

In the absence of any licensing requirements for leasing companies in Colorado, there was nothing to prevent the resilient Burnett from immediately creating a new employee leasing firm, PROSERA, and transferring many of the former clients from ERS and NSA to the new company. PROSERA was a full-service leasing firm that provided health benefits and workers' compensation and handled employees' tax deductions. In a legitimate labor leasing operation, premiums for health benefits are established on the basis of actuarial studies that estimate, given the number, age and medical histories of employees, the funds necessary to pay medical claims and administrative costs. PROSERA's health and workers' compensation plans, according to federal investigators, were not backed by any such studies, and all employees were charged a flat fee of $111 a month, regardless of whether they opted for the medical coverage or not. This rate was set far below what other leasing firms could offer to attract employer clients looking for a bargain. But with premiums set so low, the fund could never remain solvent.

The collapse of PROSERA was inevitable, and in March 1997 Burnett filed for Chapter 11 bankruptcy protection for the firm. In a civil suit filed the following November, the U.S. Department of Labor sought to have Burnett legally prohibited from participating in any ERISA plans in the future. As part of that suit, federal authorities presented evidence showing that PROSERA had failed to pay $762,000 in federal and state taxes. Moreover, the firm's collapse left employees with $375,000 in unpaid medical claims, which Burnett had originally claimed was the result of large numbers of "false claims" presented by employees. He later changed his story, attributing the problem to a "computer systems crash."

Federal investigators had another explanation—Burnett and his colleagues had illegally diverted the funds for their own personal use. Between April 1994 and April 1997, PROSERA took in $1,429,130 in health insurance and workers' compensation premiums, but only paid out $950,814 in claims. The remainder went into Burnett's pocket. In addition, Burnett used PROSERA funds to make loans totaling over $650,000 to companies under his control, loans that were never repaid.

Federal authorities charged that Burnett used these monies to enrich himself, his family members, and business associates. The company's funds, for example, were used to pay for $130,000 in charges made by Burnett's wife at such stores as Lord & Taylor, Victoria's Secret, and Eddie Bauer. The leasing company owner also allegedly spent $122,000 of the firm's money to purchase or lease automobiles for various family members, including a BMW and a Mercedes for himself. An additional $30,000 went to pay for landscaping at his home.

Burnett's exploits demonstrate the consequences of the failure to enact uniform regulations over employee leasing firms and their operators. Given his history, somebody like Jerry Burnett should never have been allowed to set up a labor leasing firm in Colorado, or any other state, and permitted to sell health insurance under the guise of being an ERISA, single employer plan. In fact, federal authorities claimed that PROSERA's benefits plan was not a single employer plan but a multiple employer welfare arrangement (MEWA) because each "participating employer who enrolled in the MEWA on behalf of its employers established a separate ERISA covered plan whose assets were, or should have been, held by the Trust." [32] However, as is the problem in most cases involving fraud in employee leasing firms, this determination was made only *after* the company had failed and left hundreds of workers with unpaid medical claims.

OTHER PEOPLE'S MONEY

There is nothing new about business owners giving into temptation and dipping into their employees' pension funds or diverting money withheld from their checks for income taxes. But it often takes years of honest, hard work to rise to a position where such opportunities exist. The owners of employee leasing companies, by contrast, can gain access to large amounts of "other people's money" in a matter of months or even weeks. This immediate access to large amounts of cash opens the door to a variety of scams that involve the embezzlement of employee funds.

Another fundamental difference exists between legitimate business owners and employee leasing operators. Very few business owners seek to embezzle the funds withheld from employee paychecks because they have an interest in keeping their businesses afloat, a goal that would be jeopardized if it were to become known or even suspected that they were stealing from their employees. Whatever larcenous impulses a business owner might have are restrained by a desire to maintain the long-term stability of his or her business. The owners of employee leasing firms, by contrast, face no such restraints on their behavior. They have the same access to employee paychecks as do business owners, but no material stake in the continued success of their clients' companies. This basic fact, combined with the largely unregulated nature of the industry, makes employee leasing companies ideal vehicles for stealing money from workers' paychecks.

This book has focused on the theft of health insurance premiums, but unscrupulous leasing company owners can just as easily steal pension contributions or income tax payments from their employees. The following cases illustrate the diversity of opportunities and the monetary returns available in employee leasing schemes.

In November 1997, 35-year-old Richard Dvorak was indicted by a federal grand jury on charges that he cheated the IRS out of $13 million in tax payments. Dvorak was the owner of a Rhode Island employee leasing firm that provided employee benefits and took care of tax deductions for 10,000 employees at 100 companies in New England. Instead of turning employees' withheld taxes over to the IRS, Dvorak allegedly used the money to fund a lavish lifestyle that included a $3 million Newport mansion; a $600,000 horse farm in Connecticut; weekend cruises aboard a chartered 143-foot yacht, at $55,000 per charter; and a fleet of Ferraris, Bentleys, Porsches, and Mercedes Benzes. A Texas insurance company that provided workers' compensation insurance for Dvorak's leased employees also claimed that Dvorak pocketed $324,000 in workers' compensation premiums paid by employers.[33]

On June 17, 1996, 62-year-old Ralph Corace of Hempstead, New York, pleaded guilty to charges that he embezzled $2.7 million from a 401(k) pension plan sponsored by his company, Job Shop, an employee leasing firm that employed primarily engineers and technical consultants who worked at high-tech firms across the country. An estimated 700 of his employees lost money in the scheme.[34] While many employee leasing schemes have targeted low-wage workers, this case illustrates that as more large corporations discover the benefits of employee leasing, more middle-class professionals may experience the down side of this new industry.

A Florida grand jury, in November 1997, charged two owners of a Palm Beach leasing firm with misclassifying employees and underreporting their payroll to avoid paying more than $800,000 in workers' compensation premiums.[35] The Florida Department of Insurance estimated that workers' compensation fraud resulted in $200 million in losses each year in Florida and that employee leasing firms were responsible for much of that fraud.[36]

In January 1996, the IRS charged that Mark Crawford, president of a Corpus Christi, Texas, employee leasing firm had engaged in a "tax pyramiding" scheme in which he failed to turn over more than $900,000 in withheld taxes to the government.[37] Five months later, Crawford would be charged with murder in a bizarre case in which a former business partner who had been involved with Crawford in a complex scheme involving a California MEWA was found asphyxiated in a metal tool box.[38]

In July 1997, the IRS filed a lien against the former president of Eeleasco, an Albany, New York, employee leasing firm that declared bankruptcy in 1993, leaving some 4,000 leased employees stranded. The IRS claimed that Eeleasco failed to pay more than $6.44 million in taxes over a three-year period. The former vice president of the company was sentenced in 1995 to serve two years in prison for his part in the tax evasion scheme.[39]

The five above schemes are but a few of the reported cases of employee leasing frauds. Exactly how frequently crimes such as these occur is impossible to state with any accuracy because, as in most areas of white-collar crime, no public or private agency systematically collects data on these events. Yet the fact that these scams continue to occur with regularity, year after year, suggests that the ultimate source of the problem lies not in the devious minds of the individuals behind these schemes but in the very structure of the employee leasing industry itself.

CONCLUSIONS

The cases described in this chapter reveal how easy it is for white-collar criminals to start employee leasing firms with little or no cash investment of their own (the only investment made by the principals in AWF was an initial capital contribution of $11,000) and within a very short time have access to large sums of money. The unregulated character of the employee leasing industry allows the operators of these firms, unlike licensed insurers, to operate health insurance plans with no minimum capital assets to provide security to the plans. Because these unregulated plans do not contribute to state guaranty funds, when they fail, leased employees have few options for recovering their losses. For former AWF employees, the aggressive stance taken by Texas officials toward firms affiliated with the leasing company resulted in many medical claims eventually being paid. Most employees of fraudulent leasing firms are not so fortunate.

In schemes like Cap Staffing and AWF, time is on the side of the crooks. Like many of the other health insurance scams examined here, the life span of these two firms was short: Cap Staffing was in business for about a year and a half and AWF for less than three years. As Ponzi schemes, this was enough time for the organizations to generate huge revenues, from which insiders were able to siphon off large amounts for personal use, while paying off just enough claims to keep clients temporarily satisfied to keep the scheme running until its inevitable collapse. The short life span of the organizations effectively limited the ability of regulators to take action against them. AWF and PROSERA, for example, both declared bankruptcy before state regulators could shut them down.

Despite the evidence of widespread problems in the employee leasing industry, by June 1995, only 13 states had passed legislation requiring licensing.[40] Curiously, in a number of states where regulatory legislation failed to be enacted, the employee leasing industry itself was asking for regulation. In New York, for example, after the failure of several Albany-area leasing firms left thousands of employees with unpaid medical claims (one of which was Eeleasco), the state's Cuomo administration convened a task force to look into the problem. On the basis of hearings held around the state, in March 1994, the task force recommended legislation that would require employee leasing firms to obtain licenses and be bonded. The state's employee leasing industry representatives agreed with the recommendation. "How's a legitimate company going to live if you can't keep the bad guys out," commented the president of the New York State Employee Leasing Association.[41] But when the Cuomo administration was replaced by the Republican administration of conservative governor George Pataki in 1995, the plan for licensing was dropped.[42]

These cases also reveal a broader problem in the employee leasing industry. Leasing firm operators not only have access to employee's health insurance premiums but also to their contributions to workers' compensation, pension funds, and tax funds. This easy access to what often amounts to millions of dollars with little federal or state oversight opens the door to numerous forms of fraud that range from simple misuse to outright embezzlement.

Despite all of its problems, in 1996, the employee leasing industry was hailed as a "hot entrepreneurial field" by the *Wall Street Journal*,[43] one that was growing at a rate of 30 percent a year (in revenues and employees).[44] In 1997, *Fortune* magazine ranked Employee Solutions, a Phoenix-based leasing firm that bought Hazar after the company declared bankruptcy in 1995, as the eighth fastest-growing company in America.[45] The industry's growth was part of a larger trend toward "outsourcing" in which employers contract out many of their functions to growing legions of consultants, temporary, and part-time workers. Faced with intense global competition, many firms have opted for a form of workforce management in which they maintain a core of managers and valued workers and "take on and shed other workers as business spurts and slumps."[46] These trends have led analysts to predict the "end of work" as we know it and a "jobless future."[47]

Accompanying these trends has been a change in the traditional social contract that governed relations between employers and employees. Today, because many employers no longer feel responsible for the general welfare of those who work for them, they no longer feel responsible for supplying health insurance, pensions, or workers' compensation benefits. Employers may view these benefits as impediments to efficient "lean and mean" businesses or as social services that should be handled by some third party like the government. At the same time, in the current conservative political climate, many federal and state government officials feel that the responsibility for such welfare benefits lies with individual citizens. The concept of medical savings accounts (MSAs), in which each individual essentially sets up their own health insurance trust fund, is a clear example of this trend in policy. The problem is that MSAs may work well for the wealthy and the relatively healthy, but they put others like the working poor and those with chronic health problems at a severe disadvantage.[48]

In the contemporary environment of corporate downsizing and layoffs, old assumptions about the value of employer-employee loyalty have fallen by the wayside. The guiding workplace philosophy of the late twentieth century appears to be "every person for him- or herself." Analysts now predict that average workers will change jobs at least five times in their lifetimes, and many will change their careers more than once. Increasingly, large numbers of workers find themselves in situations similar to that of leased employees, situations in which they are no longer referred to as "employees" but are called "consultants" or "independent contractors." As the employee leasing industry illustrates, determining exactly who their employer is has become increasingly difficult for many workers.

Old expectations about job security and the stability of such important elements of compensation as employer-sponsored medical coverage and pension plans are called into question, if not dashed completely. In the future, as new entities move in to fulfill the functions once performed by traditional employers, we can expect to see more of, and new variations on, the kinds of employee benefit thefts described in this chapter.

NOTES

1 Mukul Pandya, "Employee Leasing: The Risks of Swimming in a Big Pool," *New York Times,* 11 July 1995, pp. 3–10; Timothy O'Brien, "Rise in Employee Leasing Spurs Scams," *Wall Street Journal,* 22 March 1994, p. B-1. See also, Senate Committee on Labor and Human Resources, Subcommittee on Labor, *Toward a Disposable Workforce: The Increasing Use of "Contingent Labor,"* 103d Cong., 1st sess., 15 June 1993.

2 Del Jones, "New Boss, Same Jungle: Leasing Workers Eases Load for Small Companies," *USA Today,* 20 May 1997, p. B1.

3 Senate Committee on Governmental Affairs, Permanent Subcommittee on Investigations, *Fraud and Abuse in Employer Sponsored Health Benefit Plans,* 101st Cong., 2d sess., 15 May 1990, 242.

4 Ibid., 244.

5 Ibid., 274.

6 Senate Committee, *Fraud and Abuse in Employer Sponsored Health Benefit Plans,* 302–3.

7 Ibid., 62.

8 Ibid., 59–62.

9 U.S. Department of Labor, Office of the Inspector General, *Semiannual Report of the Inspector General: April 1–September 30, 1992* (Washington, D.C.: GPO, 1992), 82.

10 L. M. Sixel, "Employee Leasing Bill Endorsed/Morales Urges Industry Reform," *Houston Chronicle,* 19 April 1991, p. 1.

11 Much of the information used in this section was obtained from court documents in the following cases: *United States v. Borgelt,* No. 95-CR-358-X (N.D. Tex. 1995); *Jenkins v. Alexander Hamilton Life Insurance*

Co. of America, No. 93-CV-0463-P (N.D. Tex. 1993); *Morales v. Hartford Life & Accident Insurance Co.*, No. 93-CV-1297-R (N.D. Tex. 1993). Further information was found in Sandra Milburn, "American Workforce: A Case Study," Texas Department of Insurance (n.d.).

12 For an empirical analysis of the relationship between asset growth and fraud in the savings and loan industry, see Robert Tillman and Henry Pontell, "Organizations and Fraud in the Savings and Loan Industry," *Social Forces* 73 (4): 1439–63 (1995).

13 Phyllis Williams and John Trimble, "Leased and Fleeced," *Dallas Observer*, 23 May 1991, p. 15.

14 *Morales v. Hartford Life & Accident Insurance Co.*, note 11 *supra*, 23.

15 Ibid., 27.

16 Laura Tuma, "Texas Moves Against Some MEWAS," *National Underwriter*, 25 April 1994.

17 Darrel Preston, "Bankrupt Leasing Firm Strikes Accord on Insurance Charges," *Dallas Business Journal*, 18 September 1992, p. 4.

18 Ibid.

19 Peter Menzies, "American Workforce to Receive $1 Million in Settlement," *Dallas Times Herald*, 21 November 1991, p. B-1.

20 Beth Ellyn Rosenthal, "What's New in Temporary Employment," *New York Times*, 16 December 1984, pp. 3–15.

21 Chris Welin, "Employees Finding New Lease on Life," *Dallas Morning News*, 4 September 1984, p. 1C

22 Robin Robinson, "Employee Leasing Company Avoids Pitfalls," *Tulsa World*, 30 September 1990, p. G-1.

23 In California, as in most other states, employers are required to protect their employees from the costs of work-related illnesses and injuries by purchasing workers' compensation insurance. About half of all California employers purchase their workers' compensation insurance from the State Compensation Insurance Fund, a state agency. As mentioned earlier, the premiums paid by employers are determined by the number of their employees, the nature of the jobs they perform, and the employers' "loss experience." On the basis of its employees' history of accidents and illnesses, a firm receives an "experience modification rate," which causes their monthly premiums to increase or decrease. A company with no history of accidents or injuries (for example, a new company) would receive an "experience modification rate" of 100 percent, the minimum. A company with a history of extensive injuries would receive a rate that could be several times higher, requiring it to pay substantially more for its workers' compensation insurance.

According to court documents, in the 1980s John Junk, who had been the mayor of Carson, California, in 1969 and 1970, owned an employee leasing firm called the Pacific Labor Exchange (PLE). In 1986, PLE was forced to shut down after it received an experience modification rating of 309 percent because of a number of serious injuries sustained by its employees. Almost immediately after shutting down PLE, Junk set up two new leasing firms, the Western Labor Exchange (WLE) and the American Labor Exchange (ALE), for which he arranged to obtain workers' compensation insurance through a third employee leasing company, Harbor Operations Group, run by Howard Laird and his wife, Alyce.

Laird was able to get a very good deal from the state on workers' compensation insurance by blatantly lying on his application for insurance. He told the state that Harbor was a small trucking company with 12 employees, not an employee leasing firm. He also failed to mention to the state the WLE and ALE employees, who were employed by trucking companies, liquor and convenience stores, and small manufacturing companies. When he turned in his monthly reports to the state he reported a total payroll of $2.1 million a year, when in fact Harbor's annual payroll was $13.4 million. As a result of these misrepresentations, between roughly December 1986 and October 1987, Harbor paid the state only $279,000 for workers' compensation insurance rather than the $980,000 it should have paid.

In early 1988, officials at the state insurance fund decided to audit Harbor after they noticed an unusually high number of claims coming in from a company that supposedly had relatively few employees. In response, Laird and Junk shut down Harbor and started a new leasing firm, the Shannon Group. The entrepreneurial pair did not have to beat the bushes looking for clients for their new company; all they did was send letters to the employees of WLE and ALE informing them that they were now employed by Shannon. To disguise the connection between Harbor and Shannon, Laird's wife was made the secretary and chief financial officer of Shannon, using her maiden name, A. Lavon Good; a friend of Laird's, Thomas Walsh, was made the titular head of the company.

Walsh then went to the state insurance fund and applied for workers' compensation insurance for the Shannon Group. In his application he stated that Shannon employed 10 warehousemen, 5 clerical employees, and 3 truck drivers, with an estimated payroll of $220,000.

State insurance fund analysts must have had a difficult time squaring the $220,000 with the $2.3 million in gross annual payroll that Shannon reported later in its monthly reports. And even that was a gross underrepresentation of its true payroll, which exceeded $20 million a year! As a result of these flagrant misrepresentations, Shannon's owners paid only a fraction of the true amount the company owed the state. In the process, they also ripped off their clients. Of the $1.6 million that employers paid them for workers' compensation insurance, they sent the state only $335,000.

This scheme—creating new employee leasing firms, stealing workers' compensation premiums from clients and the state, then shutting down the firms when state regulators became suspicious—worked so well that over the next couple of years, Laird, Junk, and their associates would do it several more times. In late 1988, they shut down Shannon and rolled their employees into a new firm, Central Systems. In the fall of 1989, they created Admiral Systems, which only operated for two months, but in that short period managed to rip off clients for over $50,000.

Laird and Junk, along with Anderson, were indicted on federal charges and in 1996 were sentenced to prison. *United States v. Laird,* No. 93-CR-1085 (C.D. Cal. 1993).

24 Ibid.

25 Darrell Preston, "Regulation Designed to Stop Rebirth of Failed Leasing Firms," *Dallas Business Journal,* 29 August 1993, p. 1.

26 O'Brien, "Rise in Employee Leasing Spurs Scams," p. B-2.

27 Douglas McCleod, "Federal Investigation Targets Leasing Firm," *Business Insurance,* 28 February 1994, p. 3.

28 Ibid.

29 *Hazar, Inc. v. Anderson,* No. 960087 (Super. Ct., County of San Francisco 1994).

30 *United States v. Laird,* note 23 *supra.*

31 Much of the following discussion is based on documents filed in *Herman v. Burnett,* No. 97-CV-2423 (D. Colo. 1997).

32 Ibid., 2–3, "Complaint."

33 Tom Mooney, "Free-Spending Mystery Man Awaits Trial in Huge Tax Case," *Providence Journal,* 30 November 1997, p. A1.

34 Emily Baker, "Men Who Fell Victims to Fraud Now Wary," *Dallas Morning News,* 29 July 1996, p. 1A.

35 "Six More Nabbed in Statewide Fraud Probe," *PR Newswire,* 1 December 1997.

36 John McKinnon, "Officials Plan Fraud Probe in Workers' Comp Market," *Wall Street Journal,* 30 April 1997, p. A1.

37 U.S. Attorney's Office, Southern District of Texas, "IRS Moves to Stop Tax Pyramiding by Employee Leasing Firm," press release, 11 January 1996.

The Mark Crawford story goes far beyond the problems between his leasing firm and the IRS. In 1997, Crawford stood trial on charges that he murdered a former business partner with whom he was allegedly involved in a scheme to rip off a California MEWA called Mid-Valley Trust. Crawford owned an insurance company, Viking Insurance, which had contracted with Mid-Valley to provide health insurance to the MEWA's clients but which failed to pay some $500,000 in medical claims. Jerry

Bier, "Texas Murder Saga Has Fresno Connection," *Fresno Bee,* 25 May 1997, p. B1. After Mid-Valley's owners, who were themselves later indicted on federal charges of embezzlement, terminated their contract with Viking, they signed a contract with the soon-to-be defunct International Professional, Craft, and Maintenance Employees Association (IPCMEA) Trust, a Chicago-based "union" fund, to provide their clients with health benefits (see Chapter 5).

38 Scott Parks, "South Texan Rose Quickly and Fell Hard," *Dallas Morning News,* 15 July 1996, p. 1A.

39 "IRS Says Ex-CEO Owes Millions," *Electric Times Union* (Albany, N.Y.), 10 July 1997, p. E5.

40 Pandya, "Employee Leasing."

41 Joe Ross Edelheit, "Did You Hear About the Industry That's Asking to Be Regulated?" *Newsday,* 22 August 1993, p. 75.

42 James Denn, "Company Failures Fuel Calls for Tighter Controls," *Electric Times Union* (Albany, N.Y.), 10 September 1995, p. B3.

43 Roger Ricklefs, "Worker Staffing Becomes a Hot Entrepreneurial Field," *Wall Street Journal,* 4 June 1996, p. B2.

44 Jones, "New Boss, Same Jungle."

45 Lixandra Urresta, Jeanne Lee, and Shaifali Puri, "America's Fastest Growing Companies," *Fortune,* 29 September 1997, p. 86.

46 Peter Kilborn, "New Jobs Lack the Old Security in a Time of 'Disposable Workers,'" *New York Times,* 15 March 1993, p. 1A.

47 Jeremy Rikfin, *The End of Work* (New York: George Putnam, 1995); Stanley Aronowitz and William DiFazio, *The Jobless Future* (Minneapolis: University of Minnesota Press, 1994).

48 Edwin Chen, "Savings Plan May Reshape U.S. Health Care Financing," *Los Angeles Times,* 22 April 1996, p. 1.

Bogus Labor Unions

I N 1947 Congress passed the Labor Management Relations Act, better known as the Taft-Hartley Act. A landmark in labor legislation, the act granted labor unions the
right to establish trust funds "for the benefit of employees,
their families and dependents, for medical or hospital care,
pensions on retirement or death of employees, compensation
for injuries or illness resulting from occupational activity."[1]
The law thus allowed labor unions to offer health insurance
to their members as part of a package of benefits. With the
passage of ERISA in 1974 and the Erlenborn amendments in
1983, Congress made it clear that these labor union plans were
to be exempt from state regulation. ERISA was enacted in part
as an effort to control the misuse of pension funds by corrupt
union officials and others. But by the 1980s, unscrupulous
labor organization officials discovered other funds could be
plundered from union coffers without their going through the
time-consuming process of infiltrating a legitimate union to
embezzle union funds. With remarkable ease, the thieves could
create their own unions and begin immediately siphoning off
members' contributions for their own personal enrichment.

These innovations in fraud were at the center of a series of
related schemes that began in the late 1980s and ultimately

resulted in tens of millions of dollars in losses to thousands of unwitting victims across the country.

THE ODYSSEY AND LEGACY OF WILLIAM LOEB [2]

The tale begins in July 1988 on Long Island, New York, when William Loeb, a 46-year-old former union organizer, and Helen Piasecki established Consolidated Local 867 by filing an LM-1 form—a form required of all new labor organizations—with the U.S. Department of Labor. Loeb had extensive experience with labor unions and was well aware of the ease with which new labor organizations could be created. His checkered background included involvement with several labor organizations with reputed ties to organized crime. Loeb was reportedly involved in the murder of a Teamsters official in Miami in 1973 but received immunity from prosecution in exchange for his testimony.[3] In 1977, he was convicted of "cheating" in Florida in connection with a football ticket scalping scheme, and eight months later he was sentenced to four years in prison on perjury charges.[4]

Despite being neither a consolidation of anything or the eight hundred and sixty-seventh of anything, Consolidated Local 867 was a bona fide labor organization, at least on paper. Soon thereafter, Loeb and Piasecki created the Consolidated Welfare Fund, an ERISA-defined employee benefit plan, to provide health insurance benefits and a pension fund for union members. Loeb and his associates then began an aggressive campaign to enroll individuals in the new union in New York and other states.

Local 867 was not a labor union in the conventional sense. Members did not share a common occupation or participation in a common industry. The union did not engage in collective bargaining with employers or represent members in grievance proceedings. There were no mechanisms for conducting strikes or boycotts. Instead, the organization was set up solely for the purpose of marketing health insurance, receiving dues payments, and establishing retirement funds.

Consolidated was able to establish a member base because of a recent trend among labor organizations to extend union membership to "associate members." In the mid-1980s, several national labor unions, including the AFL-CIO, attempted to shore up declining union rolls by offering associate memberships to individuals "not employed in an organized bargaining unit." Under these programs, persons not covered by union contracts could still obtain direct benefits from the union in exchange for the payment of annual dues.[5] Relying on this strategy, Loeb was able to sign up new members to his labor organization regardless of their occupation; in fact, one need not have been employed to become a dues-paying member. Eventual members included doctors, lawyers, butchers, realtors, the owners and employees of a home decorating store, a jeweler, a charter boat captain, and several church ministers.

The key to Consolidated's early success lay in the fact that Loeb was able to negotiate a contract with New York–based Empire Blue Cross Blue Shield to provide health insurance to Local 867's members. Empire had previously provided insurance for a number of legitimate New York labor unions. With the backing of Empire, Loeb began mailing out brochures offering Blue Cross coverage to individuals across the country. The rates offered were considerably lower than those offered by private insurers: major medical coverage with a $200 deductible and payments of only $130 per month for an individual and $267 for a family. Moreover, enrollment was open to virtually anyone without regard to preexisting medical conditions. Thus, the plan was extremely attractive to individuals who had trouble obtaining health insurance because they could not afford it or because of preexisting conditions that prevented them from obtaining coverage from other insurance carriers.

Within two years, acting through an extensive network of brokers and sub-brokers, Consolidated had signed up over 9,000 members, each of whom paid monthly union dues in addition to their health insurance premiums, and many of whom contributed additional funds to the union's pension fund. At its peak, Consolidated was taking in hundreds of thousands of dollars a month.

In early 1990, officials at Empire began complaining to Loeb that he was marketing his plan outside of New York, the only state where Empire was licensed to sell insurance, and asked him to stop. Loeb refused, and in June of that year he stopped making payments to Empire and informed his members that Consolidated was now self-insured, meaning that their premiums were the only source of funds to cover medical claims. Empire responded the next month by canceling Consolidated's policy, retroactive to April 1990, and filing a civil suit against Consolidated and its trustees. In December 1990, a federal judge removed Loeb from his position of control at Consolidated.

In the months that followed, Consolidated's members discovered that it was increasingly difficult to get their health claims paid. Among Consolidated's victims was a middle-aged Santa Barbara couple who were forced to sell their home to help pay the $200,000 cost of bypass surgery the husband underwent, expenses they thought their policy with Consolidated covered.[6]

In June 1991, the U.S. Department of Labor filed a civil action against Consolidated and related entities alleging violations of ERISA.[7] In December, a federal judge ordered the union and welfare fund to be dissolved and appointed an independent fiduciary to oversee the distribution of the fund's remaining assets. It was discovered that the health insurance fund had less than $250,000 in assets to cover *$10 million in unpaid health claims*. What happened to the millions of dollars taken in by Loeb and his associates became the basis for a morass of civil suits and, eventually, criminal prosecution.

In the wake of Consolidated's collapse, investigators discov-

ered a complex series of illegal payoffs, kickbacks, and embez-
zlements. To start, they learned that to maintain his contract
with Blue Cross, Loeb had bribed a key employee at Empire,
paying him off with $3,600 in cash and limousine-chauffeured
junkets to Atlantic City, complete with prostitutes, gambling
chips, and free drinks. Prosecutors later alleged that the employee reciprocated by providing Loeb with a letter on Blue
Cross stationery authorizing Consolidated to sell health insurance outside of New York.

Federal prosecutors would also charge that Loeb had illegally transferred money from the welfare fund's accounts to
himself on numerous occasions. Loeb, an inveterate gambler,
often used these funds to pay off debts at casinos. On one occasion, he had $20,000 transferred from one of the fund's
bank accounts to him in Puerto Rico, where it was placed into
an account at the Sands casino. On another occasion he had
the investment firm Prudential-Bache sell $50,000 worth of se-
curities held by the welfare fund and send the proceeds to him
at the Sands, where he used the money to pay off another gambling debt.

These gambling junkets were part of the high-flying lifestyle
that Loeb enjoyed while at the helm of Consolidated, all at the
expense of the union members. On a trip to southern California in the summer of 1990, ostensibly to look for West Coast
offices for the union, he demanded to be picked up at the air-
port by a limousine driven by a female driver and stocked with
Dom Perignon champagne ("I only drink the best," Loeb explained). The driver, one Rosanna Dardon, who introduced
herself as a "full-service chauffeur," would help Loeb with
more than transportation. On her suggestion, Loeb checked
into the opulent Belair Hotel, where his $2,062 bill was paid
for with union funds. She later accompanied Loeb on a pri-
vately chartered helicopter to Catalina Island, a flight that
took less than an hour and cost $1,295. While on the island,
the pair spent $1,070 for a two-night stay at an expensive ho-
tel and $770 to pay for a chartered fishing boat, which Loeb
would later claim on his expense account was a business meet-

ing with persons who were not even on the island. The Catalina trip was the beginning of an intimate relationship between
Loeb and Dardon that led to her being placed on the union's
payroll at an annual salary of $20,000. In July 1990, as their
relationship blossomed, Loeb and Dardon purchased a cus-
tomized 1990 Cadillac Broughan stretch limousine, that federal prosecutors later described as including "a white leather
interior, bar, built-in champagne cooler, remote control TV
and VCR, power moonroof, and full privacy separator between the driver and passenger compartments." The limousine
and all of its accessories were paid for with $60,368 of Local
867's funds. Soon, Loeb and Dardon were sharing a Malibu
beach house—paid for, of course, by the union. Loeb even
used union funds to pay $5,000 to an attorney to handle a
domestic proceeding involving Dardon's former husband in
Arizona.

On a gambling junket to Las Vegas during Super Bowl
weekend, Loeb ran short of money. No problem. He simply
called one of Consolidated's brokers in Arizona and asked him
for a loan. The broker, afraid that if he did not come through
with the loan he would lose Consolidated's business, hand
delivered $10,000 in cash to Loeb in Las Vegas. Later Loeb
would repay the broker with a check from the union's account.

Loeb was also later charged with accepting kickbacks from
the firms that marketed Consolidated's health plan. One of
these was H.I.G. Associates, run by Harvey I. Glick, who also
operated a sub-broker in Arizona known as Diversified Health
Concepts (DHC). In an arrangement that proved profitable for
both men, for every individual or family that DHC enrolled in
the union's health plan, Glick paid Loeb $5. During one eight-
month period, these payments totaled $152,475. At the same
time, Glick earned over $1 million in commissions for signing
up new union members.[8]

Another element of Consolidated's scheme involved persuading union members to contribute to a retirement fund.
The fund had stiff vesting requirements, with members eli-

gible to receive partial payments only after contributing for six years and full payments after ten years. Brokers were instructed to seek "high turnover" employees for the retirement fund, those who would likely fail to meet these requirements and forfeit their contributions to the fund.

Federal prosecutors would claim that, in total, Loeb illegally diverted nearly $500,000 from Local 867's coffers.

Loeb on the Lam

Many of the above crimes were cited in a 14-count indictment that a federal grand jury handed down against Loeb and Piasecki in October 1992.[9] The following January, while under indictment, Loeb was arrested and charged with assaulting his girlfriend, Dardon. The next month he was again arrested and charged with jury tampering when he allegedly threatened to kill Dardon if she testified against him.[10] However, when she testified at his jury tampering trial she claimed that her cuts and bruises were the result of a domestic dispute that was unrelated to Loeb's fraud charges, and Loeb was reluctantly acquitted by the judge hearing the case. In March 1993, Loeb agreed to plead guilty to two counts in the indictment and requested to have his sentencing hearing postponed until September of that year. He was released on a $300,000 bond secured by his elderly mother's home and placed on 24-hour electronic monitoring.

The potential forfeiture of his mother's house, however, did not prevent Loeb from devising several elaborate schemes to avoid incarceration. In April 1993, he obtained a voter registration card in the name of "Craig Brenner," his first wife's son from a previous marriage. With that identification card, he was able to obtain a New York City Food Stamp and Public Assistance identification card under Brenner's name but with Loeb's picture on it; a New York State Department of Social Services Benefits identification card; and a birth certificate in the name of Craig Brenner. With these documents in hand,

Loeb went to a post office and filled out an application for a passport. Despite these elaborate preparations, he never obtained the fake passport.

After his first flight attempt failed, Loeb devised another plan to escape imprisonment. On August 5, 1993, a month before his scheduled sentencing hearing, Loeb took a plane from New York to Phoenix and then caught a connecting flight to Bullhead, Arizona, where he rendezvoused with Dardon and their newborn child. Apparently reconciled, he and Dardon immediately set up living arrangements (under considerably less auspicious conditions than they had previously enjoyed), applying for food stamps and welfare benefits. On September 12, 1993, he and Dardon were arrested in their motel room by federal agents and returned to New York. On December 10, 1993, Loeb was finally sentenced to 71 months in prison and ordered to pay $494,000 in restitution.

National Council of Allied Employees

William Loeb was hardly the type to be deterred by a few setbacks. In January 1991, one month after he was forced out of Local 867 but two years before he eventually pleaded guilty to two federal criminal offenses, Loeb created another union, the National Council of Allied Employees (NCAE), headquartered in Glen Head, New York. The next month he created the NCAE Welfare Fund and the NCAE Pension Fund. With the NCAE, Loeb and associates began utilizing a new strategy that gave them quicker access to a nationwide market; they began "franchising" their health fraud schemes by chartering local affiliates. Within months of NCAE's creation, at least four new locals were established. Local 444 was chartered in January 1992 and headquartered in Simi Valley, California. Local 412, operated by a former Consolidated trustee, was established in Phoenix, Arizona. Local 555 was set up in Encino, California, and immediately began marketing its health plan in California, Florida, Texas, and other states. Local 615 was headquartered in Tempe, Arizona.

These local affiliates were part of a confusing tangle of organizations and individuals whose goal was to market health insurance to unsuspecting victims around the country who were desperate for medical benefits. Of course, the rates charged were so low that the plans had no chance of survival. The complexity of these organizations and their interconnections was an integral part of the scheme as it served to confuse both policyholders and regulators about the true nature of the scheme. As an attorney in a later class action suit against the scheme's principals put it:

This case, while factually simple, has been made complex by the number of parties, alter egos and acronyms involved. This shell game was, from the inception, an artifice constructed by the Defendants through the creative use of generic business entities called "trusts," "associations," and "billing/claims administrators," which were designed to prevent individual accountability. The desired effect of the scheme by its architects was (and is) to design a labyrinthine structure that diffused responsibility and allowed unfettered collection of premiums . . . while avoiding the payment of claims.[11]

Another level of this "labyrinthine structure" consisted of "employee associations," established to market NCAE's health plan; in some instances employees were required to join one of these associations to obtain insurance. As mentioned above, two of the firms that marketed Consolidated's original health plan were H.I.G. Associates and Diversified Health Concepts (DHC), both run by Harvey Glick. In July 1990, as Consolidated was collapsing, Glick and others formed an organization named the National Association of Professionals and Executives (NAPE) and began informing Local 867's members that they could maintain their health benefits by enrolling in NAPE. DHC was headquartered in Arizona, and most of the persons enrolled in its benefit plans were residents of California and other western states.[12] Another former Consolidated trustee established a similar organization creatively named the Council for Recreation, Energy, and Tourist Enrichment (CREATE) and also began rolling former Consolidated clients into its health plan. Within a few months, NAPE and CREATE merged to form the Western Businessmen's Association (WBA).[13]

The health plans sponsored by the Consolidated Welfare Fund and the NCAE were also marketed by insurance brokers and agents who established their own multiple employer welfare arrangement (MEWA) trusts. One of these was Benefits Administrators Trust (BAT), operated out of Fort Mitchell, Kentucky, by Anthony ("Tony") Huelefeld. Huelefeld had a long history of involvement with employee benefit plans.[14] Along with his wife, Huelefeld operated several MEWAs that ultimately went bust, leaving thousands of enrollees with unpaid claims. For a number of unsuspecting victims, Huelefeld's MEWA plans were the last stop on a journey through the world of bogus health plans that began when they signed up as members of Consolidated Local 867.

Another insurance broker who figured prominently in the scheme was Ronald Loetz, who, in early 1990, created the American Family of Business Trusts, which included the American Benefit Trust (ABT), headquartered in San Ramon, California. Loetz used ABT as a vehicle to defraud former Consolidated policyholders. He advertised his plan as fully insured by Lloyds of London, when in truth, Loetz had only obtained very limited coverage from Lloyds, and even that coverage was eventually withdrawn.[15] Loetz's agent marketed ABT's health plan in California, Florida, Georgia, Ohio, and Texas, among other states. Between February 1990 and March 1991, ABT collected approximately $5.8 million in premiums from 8,000 employee members. By April 1994, ABT had stopped paying claims, leaving policyholders with approximately $3.7 million in unpaid medical bills. In 1995, the 47-year-old Loetz was charged in a 35-count federal indictment that claimed he had illegally diverted approximately $300,000 of these funds to himself.[16] In 1996, he was convicted on all counts, and the next year was sentenced to serve seven and a half years in prison.

A Road Map

The intricate mosaic of unions, locals, employee associations, trusts, brokers, and agents that comprised the Loeb/NCAE schemes gets very confusing. To help keep it all straight, the various organizations and their lineages are presented in the figure on page 116. Displayed this way, one gets a better sense of how these semiautonomous groups formed part of a larger net-work of illegal organizations. It will later be argued that this network represents a form of organized crime that in some ways resembles traditional organized crime groups but in other ways represents a newer approach to criminal enterprise.

Offshore Connections

In Chapter 2, we saw how operators of fraudulent MEWAs were able to temporarily evade the scrutiny of regulators by claiming to be fully insured by unlicensed insurance companies based in Caribbean countries. The financial soundness of these offshore insurers was difficult to determine, but on paper they had the appearance of legitimate insurance companies. Offshore insurers also figured prominently in the Consolidated/NCAE schemes. The involvement of these questionable foreign entities (in many instances, the same ones that were involved with bogus MEWAs) added yet another level of complexity to an already complicated scenario.

NCAE's Local 555 offered health benefits through an Ohio-based organization, the National Health Foundation, and was reinsured by two offshore insurers that were under investigation by state regulators for other violations. From May through October 1992, Local 555's health plan was reinsured first by Tiberian Insurance Company, domiciled in the British West Indies, and Avalon Insurance Company, Ltd., domiciled in Bermuda, and later by Provident Capital Indemnity Ltd., domiciled in the Turks and Caicos Islands.[17] All three of these unlicensed offshore insurers were eventually placed on the

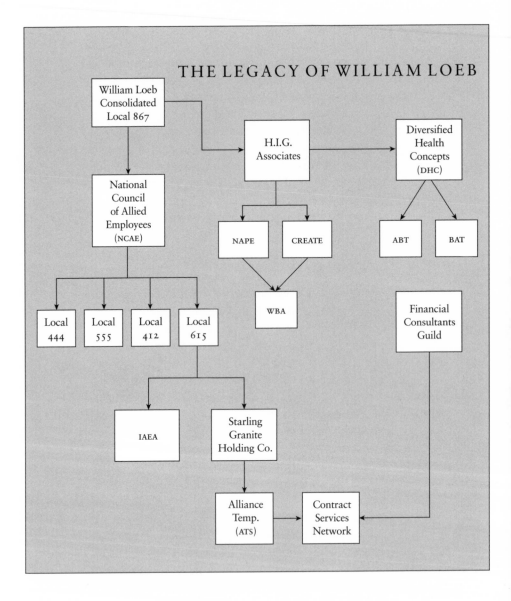

THE LEGACY OF WILLIAM LOEB

California Department of Insurance's list of unacceptable non-admitted carriers and prohibited from doing business in the state.[18]

Employees who signed up as members of NAPE/CREATE were told that their insurance was being provided by a series of offshore insurers, whose names have cropped up again and again over the years in numerous investigations of insurance fraud. One of these was the Old American Insurance Company, the same scandalous offshore insurer described in Chapter 2 that was created in the 1980s by the notorious insurance swindler Alan Teale. Another was First Assurance and Casualty Company, Ltd. of the Turks and Caicos Islands, which in April 1993 the California Department of Insurance placed on its unacceptable list after determining that many of the assets listed in First Assurance's financial reports were of questionable value. Among these was a $3 million bond issued in Texas by the St. Paul Baptist Church. California regulators were unable to verify the existence of either the church or the bond.[19]

Legal Skirmishes

Just as MEWA scam artists had, the promoters of these sham unions often turned to the courts with claims of ERISA preemptions when confronted by state regulators who sought to shut them down. In the spring of 1992, Local 555 and other NCAE locals were hit with cease and desist orders in Florida and other states. Texas filed suit against Loeb, NCAE, and several of its locals alleging that they were selling unauthorized insurance in the state without a certificate of authority.[20] NCAE responded by filing a countersuit in federal court in the Eastern District of New York, naming the states of Florida, Kentucky, Louisiana, Texas, and Virginia as defendants and claiming that the states were engaged in a concerted plan "to impede, interfere with and to disrupt the union organizing activities of [NCAE]."[21] In their suit, NCAE attorneys argued that the various states had claimed that NCAE and its locals were not legitimate union organizations and were in fact MEWAS and therefore subject to state regulation because the Secretary of Labor had not issued a finding that the plans were maintained pursuant to collective bargaining agreements. NCAE refuted this argument, claiming that "the Secretary of Labor has not established any procedure which would allow Plaintiffs to require the Secretary of Labor to make a determination or finding that said agreements are collective bargaining agreements and the Secretary has never made any such finding for this or any other union."[22] Thus, NCAE sought to rely on the loopholes in ERISA that made it difficult to determine what constituted a legitimate labor organization and thus what constituted a valid ERISA-exempted employee benefit plan.

In June 1992, the Department of Labor joined the fray by obtaining a temporary restraining order against NCAE, effectively shutting down the organization.[23] Eventually, NCAE settled with Texas, agreeing to place $406,000 into a fund to be used to pay the health claims of its victims. In March 1994, the Department of Labor closed down Local 555 and related entities permanently by filing a suit in a Los Angeles federal court.[24]

The Victims' Perspective[25]

The tangled web of organizations and individuals described so far is perhaps better understood when seen from the victims' point of view. Consider the experiences of the following individuals.

Two of the victims were John and Louise Allen.[26] John Allen was a self-employed furniture maker who lived with his wife in San Diego, California. In 1990, Allen, who had a history of heart problems, was forced to cancel his health insurance policy because the carrier would not cover treatments for any heart-related problems. In March of that year, Allen was contacted by an insurance broker who offered him a policy with Empire Blue Cross that had no preexisting conditions restrictions and would cover all medical treatments for him and his wife. Allen made out a check for the first month's premium of $252 and soon thereafter received a union card from the Consolidated Welfare Fund. In September 1990, the Allens received a letter from Empire stating that their policy had been canceled, retroactive to April, despite the fact that they had diligently sent in their premium checks. At this point, Louise Allen was told by a representative from Consolidated that she and her husband might be able to obtain coverage from H.I.G. Associates. Unaware that H.I.G. and Consolidated were intimately connected, she called H.I.G.'s offices.

H.I.G. officials told Allen that as a former member of Consolidated she and her husband would be eligible for a policy with NAPE. All they had to do was send in a check for $199 to cover the first month's premium and the same amount every month thereafter. Shortly after making their first payment in September, the Allens received a booklet that explained the NAPE plan benefits. According to the booklet, "plan benefits are being provided by American Benefit Trust, reinsured by Lloyds of London" (ABT was run by Ronald Loetz). The claims administrator was identified as Benefit Administrators, Inc. of Fort Mitchell, Kentucky (a third party administrator operated by Anthony Huelefeld).[27]

In November, the Allens received another letter from NAPE informing them that as of November 1, they were being "rolled over" into a benefit plan sponsored by Winston-Hill Assurance Company (an offshore insurer). Then on July 5, 1991, NAPE sent the Allens a letter informing them that

some problems have arisen with the health insurance program [that is, Winston-Hill's] endorsed by NAPE. . . . Because of this problem, the Board of Directors has determined that the best interest of our membership will be served by no longer endorsing the present health program. The termination of our endorsement will be July 31, 1991.[28]

On July 23, 1991, John Allen was hospitalized after suffering a heart attack. Four days later, he underwent quadruple coronary bypass surgery and was released from the hospital on August 3. His bill for the surgery and related treatments totaled $87,500. Soon thereafter, he learned that H.I.G., NAPE, and Winston-Hill all refused to pay any portion of his bill. When his wife called Winston-Hill's office, all she got was a recorded message stating that no information on health claims was forthcoming.

The operators of Consolidated and its offshoots did not focus solely on the middle-aged but also preyed on younger people. One of these was Jennifer Warner,[29] a 27-year-old Californian. In 1990, Warner lost her $50,000-a-year job as a paralegal because of a chronic kidney problem that forced her to miss work. She knew that federal law required her old insurer to continue her policy for only 18 months and that she would have to find a new policy. She also knew that finding a company that would write her a policy would be a difficult task given her preexisting kidney problem. Things seem to brighten when her insurance agent told her of a new plan that would take her, despite her medical condition. The plan was Empire Blue Cross, sponsored by the Consolidated Welfare Fund.

Warner promptly canceled her existing policy, enrolled in the Empire plan, and began sending her monthly premium checks of $474 to Consolidated. For the first few months, things were fine; her bills was paid without a problem. Shortly thereafter, she started receiving letters informing her that her insurance was being switched to insurers with addresses in the Caribbean. In December 1990, her kidney condition worsened to the point where she required surgery. She wrote to the company that sold her the policy, the Stoddard Insurance Agency, to verify that the surgery would be covered. After they told her that the procedure was covered under the policy, she went ahead with the surgery and started postoperative treatments. She would soon learn, however, that none of her bills was being paid. By June 1992, Warner's medical bills totaled $300,000, and she had no way of paying them off. Collection agencies, hospitals, and doctors began hounding her, demanding payment. She was forced to curtail her treatments because she knew she couldn't pay for them.[30]

It may have been small consolation to Warner to learn that in August 1997, J. Paul Stoddard and Jon Anton Berg of the Stoddard Insurance Agency (brokers for the Consolidated Welfare Fund) were sentenced to 37 months in prison after being convicted in federal court on charges of insurance fraud.

Jennifer Warner, the Allens, and a number of other victims were part of a class action suit filed against Loeb, Consolidated, and the various other entities involved in the scheme.[31] The suit eventually grew to massive proportions, naming over 1,000 insurance agencies and a rogues' gallery of notorious offshore insurance companies as defendants. By the fall of 1996, that suit had resulted in the collection of $8 million in judgments to cover $20 million in unpaid claims from the plaintiffs.[32] Having 40 percent of their medical bills covered is better than nothing, but the emotional and physical damages endured by the victims can never be paid for.

THE SAGA CONTINUES

One of the more remarkable aspects of these schemes was the way in which corrupt organizations continually spun off new organizations that would carry on their criminal traditions. Many of the Loeb-connected organizations became virtual magnets for insurance con artists from around the country who were drawn to them by their potential for quick profits. One of these magnetic organizations was NCAE's Local 615.

In October 1991, Local 615's head, Carleton Kirel, severed his ties with NCAE and created the United Labor Council Local 615. The organization set up its own health benefits trust and began enrolling associate members across the country. Building on the basic strategy begun by Loeb at Local 867 of creating purported unions to market health insurance, Local 615 branched off in many directions, creating offshoot locals and establishing a complex network of insurers, reinsurers, and third-party administrators. Officials at Local 615 claimed that their health plan was insured by a local insurance company, the Biltmore Insurance Group, and was marketed through an organization known as the Royal Guardian Mutual Benefit Association. Acting through a network of marketing agents and insurers, Kirel and associates were able to sign up large numbers of members in a short span of time. In one 18-month period, Local 615 took in $10 million in premiums.

Federal authorities would later allege that approximately 70 percent of that amount was diverted for the personal use of Kirel and others associated with 615's health insurance fund. Specifically, Kirel was accused of receiving payments totaling nearly $850,000 that included $46,725 paid to an automobile dealer for a new 1991 Lexus LS400, $21,123 to purchase a Ford Bronco for Kirel's wife, as well as $60,000 for a mobile home in her name. Kirel's largess also extended to his girlfriend, for whom the welfare plan's funds were used to pay for a car and travel expenses. One of Local 615's trustees, Herbert Marshall, his wife and son also allegedly received at least $545,000 from the welfare fund that was used to purchase, among other things, a new Cadillac Deville and a new Chrysler Lebaron. As a result of these extravagances, as of September 1992, Local 615's welfare fund had only $240,000 in assets to pay over $2 million in known claims, with an additional 4,500 claims whose dollar value was undetermined at that date.[33]

In 1995, Kirel and Marshall were indicted by a federal grand jury in Phoenix. They were eventually convicted and sentenced to 24- and 12-month imprisonments, respectively.[34] But their prodigy lived on.

Among Local 615's offshoot organizations were several holding companies that operated employee leasing firms run by a pair of Oklahoma businessmen, Gary Newsom and Jerome Wolfe. In the late 1980s, Newsom and Wolfe operated a leasing firm out of Oklahoma City known as Alliance Temporary Services (ATS) that provided employees with health insurance, workers' compensation, and other personnel services. The company reportedly provided these services to over 13,000 employees, primarily in Texas and Oklahoma. Newsom, who had previously been a personnel director at an Oklahoma City steel tubing manufacturer where he never earned much more than $15,000 a year, had, within three years of starting Alliance, increased his salary to $270,000 a year, moved into a 10,000-square-foot home and "assembled a corporate fleet of Jaguars, Corvettes, and Lincoln Town Cars."[35] He would eventually be accused of misappropriating more than $1.2 million from ATS.[36]

In 1990, authorities in Oklahoma and Texas prohibited Alliance from doing business in their states after they learned that Newsom and Wolfe had set up an offshore insurer in Barbados under the name Meridian Insurance (Alliance's offices in Oklahoma City were on North Meridian Street) to provide workers' compensation coverage to their clients.

After being shut down by state authorities, Newsom and Wolfe then set up a series of new employee leasing firms, controlled by two holding companies, Sterling and Granite, under the name Contract Services Network, for which they obtained health insurance from Local 615 in Arizona. Employers who signed up with one of their leasing companies would sign a collective bargaining agreement with Local 615, and their employees would become members of the union United Labor Council Local 615. Unlike the case with other labor organizations, employers had little to fear from the union. Part of the collective bargaining agreement specified that "during the life of this Agreement, there shall be no strike, stoppage of work, slow down, picketing, boycotting, lockout, or any other economic pressure or activity of any kind by either party against the other for any reason or matter, controversy or grievance, or claim of breach of contract of any kind, nature or description, between the parties hereto."

When Local 615 was on the verge of being shut down, Newsom and Wolfe were left with no insurance coverage for their leased employees, and they began looking for a new "union" for their employees. They did not have to look very long, for soon thereafter they were introduced to the head of an organization known as the Financial Consultants Guild of

America, based in Long Island, New York. Financial Consultants registered with the Department of Labor as a labor union
in August 1991. In February 1992, the Financial Consultants
Guild chartered Local 211, headquartered in Oklahoma City
and nominally headed by two of Newsom's and Wolfe's associates. With the new union in place, Newsom and Wolfe
simply made all their employees members of Local 211 as part
of a collective bargaining agreement with Contract Services
Network.

They also began signing up more employees in Oklahoma,
Texas, and other states through a hastily assembled network
of brokers. Two of these brokers—one of whom had previously sold extended new car warranties and the other, an
ex-evangelist, who had been selling prepaid funeral plans—
opened up shop in a Dallas suburb. Out of their small office,
which had no furniture or office staff, they made cold calls to
prospective clients. As one of them later described the situation, "We were just grown men sitting around on lawn chairs
making phone calls. Man we just smiled and dialed." [37]

In Texas, Contract Services' agents discovered a new source
of clients for the union's health plan: local school districts. A
recently enacted Texas law required all school districts to provide health coverage for their employees, but many of the districts could not afford the premiums demanded by licensed insurance companies. In one district, the starting salary for
teachers was $17,400 a year, while monthly health premiums
for a famlly were running around $600 a month. Not surpris-
ingly, when agents for Contract Services contacted school su-
perintendents and offered them the same coverage for only
$300 a month ($130 for individuals), they were eager to sign
up. Their enthusiasm was quickly dampened, however. Within
months of signing up with the program, school district employees found that their medical claims were not being paid,
and when they contacted Contract Services they received
vague answers. [38]

By offering cut-rate prices on health insurance to groups
who found it difficult to obtain affordable coverage, Contract

Services was able to enroll large numbers of individuals in the plan and bring in substantial revenues in a relatively short period of time. Between April 1992 and October 1993, the Network received $5.8 million in contributions. As was the case in all of the other fraudulent plans, very little of these funds was set aside to pay health claims. Much of it was diverted to the use of Newsom, Wolfe, and their colleagues. When Local 211 was eventually shut down, it had only $66,000 in assets.[39]

One of Contract Services' victims was a 34-year-old carpenter named David Bohanon. In 1992, Bohanon underwent open heart surgery and ran up a $65,000 hospital bill. He was later diagnosed with a potentially fatal, hereditary heart disease, as were two of his children. Soon thereafter, his wife, a school teacher at one of the Texas school districts that had signed up in Contract Services' health plan, learned that she had multiple sclerosis. The Bohanons assumed that their mounting medical expenses would be covered by Mrs. Bohanon's policy. They were wrong. Many of their bills went unpaid. Unable to pay the bills themselves they were forced to move to an Indian reservation in Oklahoma (Mr. Bohanon was a Choctaw) where the nearest Indian hospital was 80 miles away.[40]

Because it was run as a Ponzi scheme, Local 211 was able to stay in business only a short while before claims began to outstrip incoming revenues and the whole scheme collapsed. In November 1993, Texas obtained a temporary injunction against Contract Services Network and Local 211 that prohibited them from doing business in Texas.[41] Oklahoma authorities took a similar action.[42] These actions were only part of Newsom's and Wolfe's troubles. In August 1993, they had been convicted in Austin, Texas, on charges of defrauding the state's workers' compensation fund and were sentenced to ten years in prison. Then in June 1994, while appealing their state conviction, a civil court judge ordered the pair to pay 17 Texas school districts that had signed up with Contract Services $1.2 million in damages.[43] In March 1994, Newsom, Wolfe, and other individuals affiliated with Local 211 were hit with a tem-

porary restraining order issued by a federal judge in Oklahoma City.[44] Things went from bad to worse in 1995 when
Newsom and Wolfe were indicted by a federal grand jury in
Oklahoma City on charges of mail fraud and money laundering in connection with their operation of Alliance Temporary
Services and their offshore insurance company in 1989 and
1990.[45] After losing their appeal of the workers' compensation
conviction, the pair was ordered to begin serving sentences in
the Texas state prison at Huntsville.

Another Local 615 spinoff was the International Association of Entrepreneurs of America (IAEA), a MEWA headquartered in Irving, Texas. Unlike many of its sister organizations,
IAEA stayed in existence for a relatively long period of time.
From 1992 to 1995, the association collected more than $25
million in employer contributions in 29 states.[46] One of the
reasons for the organization's longevity was the skillful way
legal tactics were used to challenge the authority of state regulators who attempted to shut it down (see Chapter 2).

Finally, in April 1996, IAEA was seized by regulators following a civil suit filed by the U.S. Department of Labor.[47] In
that suit, federal authorities alleged that the MEWA's operators
siphoned off more than $10 million from the plan's assets.

According to the facts presented in the civil suit, IAEA was
operated more like a corrupt savings and loan than an employee benefit plan. IAEA's trustees voted to allow one of the
trustees, Ross Fuller, to use his company, Stockton Fuller, to
make investment decisions for the plan's assets. A significant
proportion of those investments appeared to be in Ross Fuller
himself; between 1992 and 1995, he received $700,000 in
compensation from the plan. He also used $30,000 of the
plan's money to purchase antique furnishings for Stockton
Fuller's offices. Fuller also made unsecured or undersecured
loans totaling over $1 million to friends and associates. In-
cluded here was a $720,000 loan made to a personal friend to
purchase a motel. That loan was never repaid. In 1993, Fuller
amended the IAEA Declaration of Trust to allow him to "play

the market" with plan assets. Fuller's subsequent dabbles in the securities market resulted in losses of $480,000 to the plan.[48]

The closure of IAEA in 1996 represented the final chapter of a long story that began in 1988 and involved a lengthy cast of characters, many of whom ended up in prison. Many of these people were not criminal masterminds. They were simply con artists with a knowledge of the insurance business who saw the tremendous potential for illicit profit in the holes created by ERISA and who took advantage of the desperation among the millions of people cast off by the legitimate insurance industry. While purported labor unions were the vehicles for their frauds, their organizations and their activities had virtually nothing in common with the operations of the many legitimate labor unions that provide health benefits to their members through sound plans that pay claims in a timely manner. Labor unions were the fraudulent vehicles of choice because William Loeb and his associates had discovered that they were remarkably easy to create and that federal law made it very difficult for anyone to challenge their legal status. But Loeb and his confederates were not the only individuals who understood the opportunities that labor organizations created for the theft of employee benefits. Another person who well understood this was an energetic New Yorker named Solomon Sprei.

"LEGAL IMPROPRIETIES" [49]

In May 1990, about the time that it was canceling the policies of Local 867's members, Empire Blue Cross was approached by Solomon Sprei, a 36-year-old Brooklyn native, who was seeking health insurance for the members of Local 1-J, a small New York chapter of the Service Employees International Union. Sprei, operating through a string of companies in Brooklyn, was the agent for the local. On paper the union's members were just the kind of people that Empire wanted to insure—relatively healthy with few preexisting conditions.

But that was only on paper. With the help of Blue Cross benefits consultant Timothy Neal, whom he bribed, Sprei submitted documents to Empire that showed the prospective policyholders to be at relatively low risk of needing medical care. Based on this data, in May 1990, Empire signed contracts to provide health coverage to Local 1-J's members.

With the Empire contracts in hand, Sprei immediately took a page out of the William Loeb playbook and began signing up individuals in the plan who had no prior connection with the union but who, on signing up in the health plan, suddenly became "associate members" of Local 1-J. These new members paid Sprei 50 percent more for health insurance than Empire was charging—which went directly into the pockets of Sprei and his associates—along with $12 a month in union dues. By signing up thousands of new associate members, Sprei was able to skim off millions of dollars in premiums.

The scheme worked so well that in September 1990, Sprei signed contracts with Empire Blue Cross to provide insurance for the members of a second union, Local 906 of the Retail Drug, Cigar, Soda and Luncheonette Employees Union. Empire had been providing health insurance to the local's members since 1965, when it covered 1,446 members; by 1990, that number had declined to less than 200. By mid-1991, however, thanks to Sprei's aggressive marketing campaign, the number of members covered by Empire had grown to more than 4,400.

Within months, Empire began receiving claims from the unions' members that were way out of line with the actuarial projections they had made based on the data Sprei and Neal had supplied. Empire officials began to smell a rat and, in May 1991, canceled their contract with Local 1-J and Local 906.

Not the type to give up on a good thing, Sprei approached other insurance companies and presented them with falsified data on claims submitted by the unions' members to Empire Blue Cross, data that showed relatively low claims charges. Based on this data, in June 1991, State Mutual Life Assurance Company of America began providing health insurance coverage to Sprei's clients. It didn't take State Mutual officials long to realize they'd been had, and they soon began to refuse payment on claims submitted by Local 1-J's members. Eventually, the company would withhold payments to 6,100 households totaling $9.3 million. State Mutual would later agree to pay only forty cents on the dollar to the individuals who had submitted those claims.

In January 1996, Sprei was indicted by a federal grand jury in Manhattan, which charged him with defrauding various insurance companies and policyholders of over $17 million. In October of that year, Sprei pleaded guilty to two counts in the indictment.

Despite the massive losses involved, the case generated little media attention until after Sprei was sentenced. Although federal sentencing guidelines required a sentence of 36 to 48 months in prison, a federal judge in Manhattan ordered Sprei to serve 18 months and pay $1.8 million in restitution. The judge was apparently influenced by a well-orchestrated campaign by Sprei's supporters to have his sentence reduced.

Solomon Sprei was a member of an orthodox Jewish community in Brooklyn known as the Bobov community (the group traces its roots back to a small town in Poland named Bobov), whose spiritual leader was an 89-year-old rabbi named Solomon Halberstam. In the period after Sprei's conviction, Rabbi Halberstam and other members of the community gave testimony and wrote numerous letters to the court attesting to Sprei's good character, his standing in the community, and his numerous good deeds. In his letter to the judge, Rabbi Halberstam wrote:

[Sprei] has admitted to me deep regret over his improper behavior. . . . This is not to dismiss that he has done wrong, but in meting out its punishment justice needs to consider the entire person.

The rabbi went on to acknowledge Sprei's "legal improprieties" but argued that sending him to prison would do more harm than good:

I dread to predict the impact [of imprisonment] on the structure of this family. His children of marriageable age will not be able to find spouses for themselves and in our community this is a devastating situation. Without their father to help them and seek out matches for them and to guarantee the financial arrangements they will be as "living orphans." Heaven forbid.

The judge in the case was apparently convinced; he referred to the letters on Sprei's behalf as "quite moving." In imposing the reduced sentence he noted, "I am persuaded that to incarcerate Mr. Sprei would wreak extraordinary destruction of a kind that never dawned on the Sentencing Commission on a number of these children." The judge was apparently less concerned about the welfare of thousands of children whose parents were stuck with unpaid medical claims as a result of Sprei's crimes.

CONCLUSIONS

It's easy to get caught up in the details of the Loeb and associates story and lose sight of the bigger picture. The details of the case study, though, serve to illustrate an important point. A fundamental feature of the form of white-collar crime under study here is its recurrent nature. These crimes represent *recombinant fraud*. This is a process in which fraudulent organizations are created, operate their schemes, collapse, then spin off new fraudulent organizations, which go on to repeat the cycle. The term *recombinant,* borrowed from genetics research, is used as a metaphor here to suggest the ever-changing mutation of organizations, each of which borrows pieces from its predecessors to pursue essentially the same goal: defrauding individuals, companies, and government programs.[50] Like a resilient virus, these organizations appear to defy control by law enforcement agencies and regulators. As soon as one fraudulent organization is shut down, another, or several, appears to take its place, often utilizing new strategies to adapt to the changed environment. Part of the strength of these organizations is their ability to combine and recombine actors from previous schemes into flexible, often far-flung, but well-coordinated networks that can move quickly across state and national borders. As one investigator put it, "these schemes are constantly evolving and we are constantly playing catch-up with the crooks."[51]

Recombinant fraud flourishes in industries like the insurance industry that are essentially information-based, need little in the way of physical equipment, and have few restrictions on geographic location. In a number of the cases examined here, when authorities would shut down a bogus health plan in one state, the operators would reopen a new organization in another state in a matter of days and begin rolling over policyholders into their new plan with few disruptions to their operations. These transitions were often transparent to enrollees in the plan, many of whom had little or no direct contact with the plan's operators and for whom the name and address of the organization were little more than parts of a letterhead on pieces of paper they received in exchange for their premium payments. One could argue that these forms of recombinant fraud will become more common as our society moves away from an economy based on industrial production and toward a service-based economy, in which financial institutions predominate.[52] In industries that are increasingly built around trust placed in abstract entities whose only product is the promise to fulfill some future financial obligation, the potential for such widespread frauds becomes ever more ominous.

The difficulties that law enforcement agents have in dealing with these forms of fraud were expressed by one state investigator in the following way:

The technology has made this a lot more difficult and also is just spreading this stuff like a virus. You know with faxes and 800 numbers they can literally be in every town in your state in two weeks and just cover more ground and also avoid mail fraud [statutes]. It's just harder to keep track of something you can't really intercept.[53]

For the traditional professional criminal, making an escape was a major problem that involved a plan to physically transport themselves and their ill-gotten gains to some safe haven—often a faraway state or foreign country—without being detected by the authorities. The white-collar criminals discussed here may represent the professional thieves of the future. For them, escape generally involves the movement of electronic devices, such as computers and computer disks that contain information about their clients, and the deployment of legal tactics that delay the efforts of law enforcement agencies to shut them down. The hide and pursue relationship between cops and crooks of the past took place largely in physical space. Today, it increasingly takes place in cyber- and legal space.

NOTES

1 29 U.S.C. § 186(c)(5)(A) (1947).

2 Much of this section is based on documents found in case files for *United States v. Loeb*, No. 92-CR-870 (S.D.N.Y. 1992). Particularly useful was the "Government's Sentencing Memorandum" for William Loeb.

3 Kevin McCoy, "Insurance Embezzler Captured," *Newsday*, 6 October 1993, p. 39.

4 *Florida v. Loeb*, No. 76-0908-c (11th Judicial Cir. of Fla., Dade County 1977); *Florida v. Loeb*, No. 78–7893 (11th Judicial Cir. of Fla., Dade County 1978).

5 Paul Jarly and Jack Fiorito, "Associate Membership: Unionism or Consumerism," *Industrial and Labor Relations Review* 43 (1990): 209–24.

6 Barry Meier, "A Growing U.S. Affliction: Worthless Health Policies," *New York Times*, 4 January 1992, p. A-1.

7 *Martin v. Goldstein*, 775 F. Supp. 649 (S.D.N.Y. 1991).

8 *United States v. Loeb*, note 2 *supra*, 13, "Government's Sentencing Memorandum"; *United States v. Glick*, No. 95-CR-0466 (E.D.N.Y. 1995).

9 *United States v. Loeb,* note 2 *supra.*

10 Ronald Sullivan, "Man Charged with Threatening to Kill a Witness," *New York Times,* 14 February 1992, p. B-3.

11 *In re* Consolidated Welfare Fund ERISA Litigation, *Bailey v. Empire Blue Cross,* 856 F. Supp. 837 (S.D.N.Y. 1993).

12 Ronald Campbell, "Unhealthy Insurance," *Orange County Register,* 26 December 1993, p. 1.

13 Ibid., 4.

14 In the late 1980s, Huelefeld also operated a series of third-party administrator firms that negotiated stop-loss insurance with licensed insurers for firms that were offering self-insurance plans to their employees. Under these arrangements, the self-insured firms would transfer funds to Huelefeld's TPAs, which in turn would make payments to the insurers for stop-loss insurance that would cover health claims over a certain dollar amount, usually $100,000. Huelefeld would later be named in a 17-count federal indictment that alleged he and his associates essentially overcharged their clients for the insurance coverage, pocketing the differences, which ran into the hundreds of thousands of dollars. Following his conviction on these charges in May 1992, Huelefeld was sentenced to serve 18 months in federal prison.

15 *United States v. Loetz,* No. 95-CR-40086 (N.D. Cal. 1995) ("United States' Pre-trial Memorandum").

16 *United States v. Loetz,* note 15 *supra.*

17 *Reich v. American Healthcare Underwriting Managers,* No. 94-1998 (C.D. Cal. 1994).

18 A. M. Best, *A. M. Best Special Report: Solvency Study of the Excess & Surplus Lines Industry,* 1996, 62–63.

19 *Bailey v. Empire Blue Cross,* note 11 *supra.*

20 *Texas v. NCAE,* 791 F. Supp. 1154 (W.D. Tex. 1992).

21 *NCAE v. Florida,* No. 92-CV-2108 (E.D.N.Y. 1992).

22 *NCAE v. Florida,* note 21 *supra.*

23 *Martin v. Loeb,* No. 92-CV-2680 (E.D.N.Y. 1992).

24 *Reich v. American Healthcare Underwriting Managers,* note 17 *supra.*

25 Much of the discussion in this section is taken from *Bailey v. Empire Blue Cross,* note 19 *supra.*

26 John and Louise Allen are pseudonyms.

27 *Bailey v. Empire Blue Cross,* note 19 *supra.*

28 Ibid.

29 Jennifer Warner is a pseudonym.

30 Edmund Sanders, "Unlicensed Firm Left Woman with $300,000 in Unpaid Bills," *Los Angeles Daily News,* 6 June 1992, p. B1.

31 *Bailey v. Empire Blue Cross,* note 19 *supra.*

32 Ibid.

33 Ibid.

34 *United States v. Kirel,* No. 95-CR-091 (D. Ariz. 1995).

35 Kevin Helliker, "Some Injured Workers Learn the Hard Way They Aren't Insured," *Wall Street Journal,* 19 March 1991, p. A18.

36 Ibid.

37 Robert Tomsho, "Health-Benefit Scams Are Alleged to Take a New Form: Unions," *Wall Street Journal,* 10 January 1994, p. A6.

38 Ibid.

39 *Reich v. Newsom,* No. 94-CV-00441 (W.D. Okla. 1994) ("Memorandum in Support of Application for Temporary Restraining Order and Preliminary Injunction").

40 Tomsho, "Health-Benefit Scams," p. A6.

41 *Texas v. Contract Services Union Local 211,* No. 93–09800 (201st Judicial Dist., Austin 1993).

42 *Oklahoma v. Newsom,* No. CJ-93-6467 (Oklahoma County District Court, Oklahoma City 1993).

43 United Press International, 16 June 1994.

44 *Oklahoma v. Newsom,* No. 93-CV-1457 (W.D. Okla. 1993).

45 *United States v. Newsom,* No. 95-CR-36-R (W.D. Okla. 1995).

46 Douglas McLeod, "Tennessee Seizes MEWA," *Business Insurance,* 29 April 1996, p. 48.

47 *Reich v. Fiore,* No. 96-CV-0347 (M.D. Tenn. 1996).

48 *Reich v. Fiore,* note 47 *supra.*

49 Sources for the discussion of Solomon Sprei include the following: Henry Gilgoff, "The Health Unsurance Crisis," *Newsday,* 9 August 1992, p. 58; Benjamin Weiser, "Judge Has His Own Take on Sentencing Formulas," *New York Times,* 14 September 1997, p. 39; *Sprei v. Empire Blue Cross/ Blue Shield,* No. 92-CV-0423 (S.D.N.Y 1992); *State Mutual Life Assurance Co. v. Retail Local 906 AFL-CIO Welfare Fund,* No. 91-CV-8575 (S.D.N.Y. 1991); *United States v. Sprei,* No. 96-CR-0029 (S.D.N.Y. 1996).

50 The term *recombinant* has been used in social science contexts by Todd Gitlin in his study of the television industry where he discusses "recombinant culture" (*Inside Prime Time* [New York: Pantheon, 1985], 75–81) and by David Stark to describe property management strategies in emerging capitalist countries ("Recombinant Property in East European Capitalism," *American Journal of Sociology* 101[4]: 993–1027 [1996].

51 Personal interview with the author.

52 Kitty Calavita and Henry Pontell, "'Other People's Money' Revisited: Collective Embezzlement in the Savings and Loan and Insurance Industries," *Social Problems* 38 (1991): 96.

53 Personal interview with the author.

Not an Insurance Company

HE preceding chapters have discussed some of the basic forms of small group health insurance fraud. The architects of these schemes took advantage of a tremendous demand for health insurance as well as legal loopholes to set up complex arrangements whose ultimate goal was to steal insurance premiums from policyholders. Common among those schemes was the promoters' claim that they were not in the business of selling insurance. This chapter takes a closer look at several variations on this strategy. It begins by examining two cases in which purported labor unions were used as the vehicles for health insurance and workers' compensation scams. Then a series of cases is examined in which putative religious organizations were used to market health insurance. Although these latter cases do not involve claims to ERISA status as do the others discussed in this book, they are similar in their denial that they are involved in the business of selling insurance; their resulting claim to exemption from state regulation represents a key to their operations.

LAWERNCE KENEMORE:
REBEL WITH A CLAUSE

William Loeb may not have been the world's most sophisticated criminal, but he planted a seed that would produce many hybrids. All of these offsprings relied on Loeb's basic strategy of creating bogus labor unions and employer groups as mechanisms for marketing health insurance outside of state or federal regulation, but often with a few new touches. Some of these hybrids grew like kudzu in the South and, like the resilient vine, proved extremely difficult to keep from spreading once they took root. One of these offshoots was an organization known as Association of Trust and Guarantee (ATG) and its founder was a smooth-talking insurance salesman named Lawernce Kenemore.

Kenemore's twist on established insurance fraud schemes was to focus on the sale of workers' compensation insurance and health insurance to the individuals who became members of his "unions." Almost all states require employers to provide workers' compensation coverage for their employees to cover the costs of injuries and illnesses sustained on the job. Like health insurance, the cost of workers' compensation coverage has skyrocketed in recent years, hitting small employers particularly hard. Kenemore and his associates took advantage of this situation to sell worthless policies to hundreds of employers across the country.

In the spring of 1993, Kenemore was running the Bestland Insurance Agency in Brea, California, where he was selling workers' compensation insurance and health insurance supplied by the United States Financial and Guarantee Association (USF&G). Kenemore had been battling with state regulators for some time claiming that his workers' compensation plan was an ERISA plan and not subject to state regulation. The state insurance department began receiving complaints from policyholders, including one, the Association of the Developmentally Disabled, that claimed Bestland failed to pay their claims after they'd paid over $90,000 in premiums.[1] On

March 30, 1993, agents from the California Department of
Insurance seized Bestland's offices and placed the firm in receivership.

In documents filed in an Orange County superior court in
October 1993, California regulators voiced a number of concerns about Bestland's operations.[2] First, Kenemore was selling
workers' compensation for an insurer that used the acronym
USF&G. Many purchasers may have confused this USF&G with
a well-known insurance company, United States Fidelity and
Guaranty, which uses the same acronym. Second, regulators
asserted that Bestland sold insurance policies under the name
CIGNA but did not forward any of the more than $40,000 in
premiums collected to the insurance giant that most people associate with that name. Third, Bestland also sold more than
60 insurance policies for a company known as People's Assurance Cooperative, despite the fact that in March 1992, the
Department of Insurance had issued a cease and desist order
against the company prohibiting it from selling its policies in
California.[3] People's claimed that its policies were backed by
Transport Risk Ltd., a purported offshore surplus lines carrier
that claimed to have its base in the Turks and Caicos Islands.
In their cease and desist order, California regulators asserted
that a major portion of Transport Risk's claimed $29 million
in assets consisted of borrowed artworks, whose value could
not be determined, as well as "$375,000 worth of Panama-
nian government bonds which have been in default for the past
four years."[4]

The California regulators were also concerned that Kenemore had apparently lied on his application for a broker's license when he answered "No" to the question "Have you ever
been convicted of a crime?" In 1983, Kenemore, while working as a part-time paramedic and insurance agent, was arrested and charged with arson, but eventually pleaded guilty
to vandalism.[5]

Not mentioned in the California regulators' documents was
the fact that Kenemore had also sold insurance for the International Association of Entrepreneurs of America (IAEA), the

Loeb spinoff multiple employer welfare arrangement (MEWA) described briefly in Chapter 4. In January 1992, Kenemore signed an agreement with IAEA to act as an agent to sell its policies. Just six months later, IAEA's principals (who would themselves be charged with fraud several years later) sued Kenemore in a Dallas district court alleging that he had misappropriated funds. The suit claimed that Kenemore had skimmed some $69,000 in premiums that should have been forwarded to IAEA.[6] Apparently, the old adage about honor among thieves is true.

The California insurance regulators concluded that "Bestland's activities are so infected with illegality that it is futile to proceed with conservation" and that liquidation of the company was the only solution.[7] Meanwhile, Kenemore was on to other things.

Three days after state regulators shut down Bestland, Kenemore formed the Association of Trust and Guarantee (ATG), a company through which he would market an employee benefits package. He then created several unions—the National Employers Trade Association (NETA) Local 101 (which ATG falsely claimed had a charter from the National Organization of Industrial Workers, an established and legitimate labor organization), the Affiliated Guilds of America, and the National Employees Trade Alliance—by filing the required forms with the U.S. Department of Labor. Next, he embarked on an aggressive campaign to market an employee benefits package to small employers in a number of states. As in the Loeb schemes, employers would sign up as members of ATG, and their employees would become members of one of the affiliated unions. Employees were then provided with benefits as part of a collective bargaining agreement between the union and the employers' association.

Kenemore advertised his plan as an innovation in employee benefits: a "twenty-four hour" plan that would provide employees with health coverage both on and off the job—health insurance as well as workers' compensation. ATG's marketing materials claimed that its program was less expensive than traditional forms of workers' compensation because as an ERISA plan, ATG was not required to contribute to state reserve funds, resulting in a savings of 10 to 50 percent in workers' compensation costs to employers. ATG's sales brochures proclaimed:

WE DO NOT SELL INSURANCE and there are no insurance premiums. . . . Our "loophole" is provided by the Federal ERISA law which is very clear that it pre-empts ALL state regulatory authority. . . . ATG is firmly committed to continue providing the finest "employee benefits package" available at affordable prices to businesses all across America. Join in the fight and promote Free Enterprise.

In September 1993, just five months after ATG was created, California regulators seized ATG's offices in Garden Grove, charging that the firm was selling unlicensed workers' compensation insurance, and sought a court order placing the company and its unions in receivership. A state judge who heard the case determined that the state had not proven its claims to jurisdiction over the putative ERISA plan and refused to issue such an order. ATG was soon back in business. Shortly thereafter, Kenemore moved ATG's headquarters to Arlington, Texas, and NETA Local 101, whose secretary-treasurer was Kenemore's son Joseph, moved to Broken Arrow, Oklahoma, a suburb of Tulsa.

From his Texas headquarters, Kenemore enlisted hundreds of sales agents to market the ATG plan across the country. Kenemore, who had a gift for rhetoric, would recruit his agents at sales meetings, where prospective ATG brokers paid $150 a head to hear an inspiring speech on the wonders of his "breakthrough" in health insurance and workers' compensation coverage and the fortunes that awaited those farsighted enough to get on the ATG bandwagon. By January 1994, Kenemore claimed to have 8,760 sales associates operating in 17 states. Federal authorities would later allege that in its short history ATG took in over $1.7 million.[8]

By late 1993, Kenemore and ATG were under increasing fire

from regulators in a number of states. On September 30, the Colorado Department of Insurance filed a cease and desist order against ATG. Less than two weeks later, while he was delivering a particularly rousing speech to a group of 40 prospective ATG marketers in Missouri, Kenemore acknowledged some of his recent legal difficulties but told the crowd: "I am selling this product in 17 states. I would like to see one of those states get me in court." At which point an official from the Missouri Department of Insurance who was sitting in the audience made his way to the podium and, as he later put it, "tried to oblige him" by handing Kenemore a court order temporarily enjoining him from selling workers' compensation insurance in the state.[9] During the next several months, regulators in Georgia, Nevada, and Utah took similar actions.

One of the states that took an active interest in Kenemore's activities was Florida. In March 1994, agents from the state's Department of Insurance attended a sales meeting sponsored by Kenemore in Orlando. During an intermission, the agents lured Kenemore outside the main meeting room with "a promise of pastries left over from another meeting" and arrested him. He was later charged with felony counts of operating an unauthorized MEWA. Those charges, however, were later dismissed by a local judge after the district attorney failed to move quickly enough on the case.

During the next year, ATG remained under siege by state and federal authorities. In the fall of 1994, a federal judge in North Carolina found Kenemore in contempt of court, and he spent two weeks in jail.[10] Things went from bad to worse in January 1995 when a Texas federal court froze ATG's assets after the U.S. Department of Labor obtained a temporary restraining order against the association.[11] But Kenemore's real troubles began on April 4, 1995, when he was named in a federal indictment in Dallas. That indictment charged Kenemore, his wife, son, and five associates with 25 counts of money laundering, mail fraud, and conspiracy to defraud. The indictment charged that Kenemore and others diverted $1.2 million of the $1.7 million paid into ATG's trust by some 294 employers. The indictment further alleged that Kenemore and his wife attempted to launder the diverted funds by transferring the money to a bank account in Antigua, West Indies, and then back into a Texas bank account.[12] A Florida regulator later described the money laundering scheme as "inept":

> The money sent through Antigua was wire transferred, creating a specific paper trail. The defendants apparently used no cleaning device such as a loan back scheme and did not attempt to mix the funds with any other cash flow. They even kept reasonably neat files describing each offshore transaction at their place of business. Meyer Lansky (reputed to be the brains in the '40s and '50s behind organized crime in America and brilliant at setting up schemes to launder and hide mob money) must be rolling over in his grave.[13]

The postindictment Kenemore/ATG story also contains a number of interesting twists. ATG's sales literature often carried an antigovernment undertone, depicting state attempts to regulate ATG as oppressive intrusions into free enterprise. These statements apparently reflected deeper political views held by Kenemore, who was a member of a right-wing political group called the Libertarian Patriots, allegedly an offshoot of the radical tax-protest group Posse Comitatus. On the day that Kenemore was to be arrested, 30 to 40 of the Libertarian Patriots staged a protest outside his Arlington, Texas, home, provoking a standoff with federal law enforcement agents. The situation was resolved when agents kicked down the door and hauled Kenemore off. Interestingly, given his political views, Kenemore, claiming that he was bankrupt, asked for and was given a court-appointed attorney. Later he dismissed the attorney and represented himself at trial.

At his trial, details of the human consequences of Kenemore's crimes were brought out. One of the employers victimized by ATG was Alliston Kilgore, the owner of five nursing homes in Arkansas and Missouri with approximately 600 employees. In July 1993, Kilgore needed to obtain workers' compensation coverage for his employees; he contacted an ATG agent who presented him with brochures describing the plan and Mr. Kenemore's "hands on" management philosophy ("yes, he returns all calls" the pamphlet cheerfully announced). The sales literature also stated that "ninety-nine percent of our customers renew their plans with us year in and year out"—a peculiar claim given that ATG had been in existence for less than six months. Kilgore was convinced and signed up with ATG, handing over a check for $39,929 for the first and last months' payments and agreeing to pay a monthly charge of $19,929 for workers' compensation coverage for his employees.[14] In August, Mary Lee Johnson,[15] a nurse at one of Kilgore's nursing homes in Arkansas, was struck in the knee by a confused resident at the nursing home where she worked. Shortly thereafter, the knee began to swell, and she experienced considerable pain. Johnson saw a physician who recommended that she see a specialist. After paying a $1,000 deductible, her employer learned that ATG would not pay her claims, and Johnson was unable to obtain the necessary treatment from a specialist. As a result, she developed a debilitating condition and eventually lost the use of her leg.

Kilgore sued Kenemore, ATG, and related entities and was awarded over $650,000 in damages by a federal jury in Arkansas. It was a hollow victory, however, because Kilgore never expected to receive any payment on the award in light of Kenemore's financial condition.

After his indictment, Kenemore gained further notoriety through the creative use of a legal tactic, the lien, against those he felt had wronged him. Kenemore placed liens on the personal assets of judges, regulators, prosecutors, and IRS agents who had taken action against him and his companies.[16] It can take many months and substantial amounts of money for an individual to have a lien removed from his or her property, regardless of the validity of the original claim. Kenemore also filed a number of civil suits against government officials. Following his indictment, Kenemore began offering seminars to instruct others, at $150 a head, on the use of the legal tactic. He became something of a celebrity among antigovernment and antitax groups, who saw his efforts as a blow against government repression. The tactic of placing liens on the property of government officials was widely used by other right-wing groups, notably the militant Freemen of Montana.[17] Kenemore's notoriety prompted the *New York Times* to give him the title "the lien king." [18]

Kenemore's use of arcane legal tactics, often flavored with bizarre antigovernment rhetoric, caused a delay in his trial of months. Acting as his own attorney, Kenemore filed numerous motions, many of which resembled those filed by the Freemen whose legal philosophy was described as a "jumble of odds and ends from the Bible, the U.S. Constitution, [and] the Uniform Commercial Code." [19] In one of his motions, Kenemore questioned the federal government's authority over him as a citizen:

Your affiant is not the creation or chattel property of any person or the corporate STATE OF TEXAS, its principals, or the United States, or any government agency whatsoever. U.C.C. 2.105. . . .

THAT it is the sincerest KNOWLEDGE, and spiritual conviction of this Affiant that slavery and peonage (Thirteenth Amendment to the Constitution for the United States of America 1787) are immoral, are violations of the First Precept of Commercial Law (a workman is worthy of his hire, "Thou shall not steal," Exod. 20:15; Deut. 5:19) that fraud, misrepresentation, nondisclosure, intimidation, deceit, concealment of material fact, lying, and treachery are morally wrong. . . .

The material facts on the indictment are totally incorrect. . . . You have a wrong address, you have me in an improper venue, I do not dwell in the Federal Zone. Thus, I am not subject to the scope and purview of those statutes, as I do not inhabit that land or do commerce under the trading with the enemy act in that jurisdiction.[20] (Emphasis in original.)

Although both the prosecutors and the judge found Kenemore's argument ludicrous, it did serve to delay the proceedings.

Kenemore's oftentimes bellicose personality was reflected in other actions. At a pretrial hearing, Kenemore's son, who had already pleaded guilty to the federal charges, testified that his father had asked him to find the home addresses of the California regulators who had investigated him, as well as the schools their children attended, "so he could get revenge."[21] The son also testified that his father had said that he would "break the legs" of a California attorney.[22] Kenemore's wife testified at her sentencing hearing that she only participated in the illegal schemes because she feared her husband's "brutal beatings,"[23] though prosecutors expressed skepticism at her claims of abuse.

On May 2, 1996, following a six-week trial, Lawernce Kenemore was convicted on all counts in the indictment. In July, he was sentenced to serve 19 years and 7 months in federal prison. His wife was sentenced to 5 months' imprisonment.

INTERNATIONAL PROFESSIONAL, CRAFT AND MAINTENANCE EMPLOYEES UNION

About the same time that Kenemore was setting up ATG, three men from Chicago were attending a seminar in Reno, Nevada, where they were learning what Kenemore already knew: that labor unions could serve as perfect vehicles to market health insurance and bring in large amounts of money in a short period of time. When they returned to Chicago, they set about putting what they had learned into practice.

In the fall of 1993, John Wolfe, Gerald Lee, and Richard Wesley, all of whom had previously worked for Chicago-area labor unions, created the International Professional, Craft and Maintenance Employees Union (IPCMEU), along with two locals: Local 1 and Local 100. They then set up a series of "employer associations" purportedly to represent the employers of the workers who would become members of the union. Following the blueprint created by Loeb and others, they then drew up collective bargaining agreements between the locals and the employer associations, which included access to a health insurance plan funded by the International Professional, Craft and Maintenance Employees Association (IPCMEA) Trust. The trust was self-insured, fully funded by employer-employee contributions.

To avoid claims that they were simply selling health insurance under the guise of a labor union, the plan was marketed to employers through a network of a dozen "service centers" located around the country. In fact, these service centers were insurance agents and brokers (both licensed and unlicensed) who marketed the plan like any other health insurance to employers around the country. The employers whose employees signed up for the plan became members of the union, often without their knowledge.

The union, the two locals, the employer associations, and the service centers all received a portion of the contributions made by employer-clients and their workers. The locals received between $8 and $15 per month per participant; the employer associations received $5 to $15 per month; and the service centers kept approximately 15 percent of all the contributions. Investigators would later determine that 40 percent of all the contribution funds were used to pay for things unrelated to the payment of medical claims. Legitimate union plans rarely expend more than 15 percent for administrative costs. And this proportion actually underestimates the amount diverted from the fund because it does not include the substantial number of medical claims that the fund failed to pay at all.

The rate schedule that IPCMEA Trust officials used to determine the employees' premiums was actuarially unsound and could never support the fund on a long-term basis. Moreover, employers were often offered rates below those listed in the schedule to induce them to sign up with the plan, a fact that further hastened the fund's inevitable collapse.

In the summer of 1996, the IPCMEA Trust did indeed collapse with unpaid medical claims estimated to total $2.5 million.

In July 1996, as IPCMEU was falling apart, two of the three original founders of the union, Wesley and Lee, joined with a former head of one of IPCMEU's service centers, James Kennelly, to form two new unions: the Professionals and Affiliates Union, Local 1, and the National Alliance of Business and Professionals, Local 100. Both of these new unions offered health plans to their members from a newly created trust, the Professional Employees and Affiliates Association (PEAA) Trust. The two new unions and their trust were set up in the same way as IPCMEU. A number of service centers and employer associations simply shifted from IPCMEU to one of the new unions.

A significant proportion of IPCMEU's clients were in California, many of them signed up by a charismatic "new age" insurance broker named Steven Gorman. Gorman ran Alternative Health Insurance, Inc., in Thousand Oaks, California, which was designated as an IPCMEU service center. He also operated an organization known as the Alliance for Alternatives in Healthcare, which was designated as an employer association for IPCMEU's health plan.

Gorman and his organizations had recently received national media attention for being in the forefront of a movement to provide health insurance plans that covered alternative medical treatments, including acupuncture, herbal medicine, chiropractic treatment, naturopathy, and traditional Chinese medicine. Gorman claimed to have provided health coverage for groups like the National Organization for Women.[24] Gorman's Alliance was promoted in health food stores and on late-night television infomercials. Through these marketing channels Gorman enrolled nearly 1,000 members in IPCMEU's health plan. The Alliance also advertised over the Internet on a web site that could be accessed via a web link to "The Age of Enlightenment Mall Services." There the philosophy of the "Alternative Health Plan" was explained:

The Philosophy of the Alternative Health Plan is that an individual should have the ability to choose treatments that encourage natural healing and prevention, while maintaining the option of conventional Western medicine, if necessary. Often, a natural approach can be more effective and harmless in eliminating disease than an allopathic approach, which may produce harmful side effects.

Treatments covered by the plan included colon therapy, herbal medicines, massage therapy, and homeopathy. In addition, "after 6 months of continuous coverage, members are eligible for 3 days of the Maharishi Ayur-Veda Rejuvenation Program at a reduced cost of $50.00 per day, if prescribed by a Maharishi Ayur-Veda physician and provided by a contracted Maharishi Ayur-Veda Medical Center."

In its electronic flyer, prospective clients were told that "the Alternative Health Plan is not an insurance policy. It is a Jointly managed Taft-Hartley Multiemployer Health and Welfare fund, which is operated in accordance with the Taft-Hartley Act and the Employee Retirement Income Security Act (ERISA)." In response to the question "Is the Alternative Health Plan Financially Stable?" posed in a "Commonly Asked Questions" section of the flyer, the following answer was provided:

Yes. Benefits for the Alternative Health Plan are provided by the International Professional, Craft and Maintenance Employees Association Trust. The Trustees that manage the trust fund have many years of experience in the administration and management of union health and welfare funds. The Trust has sufficient membership to fund the benefits offered and the Trustees have acquired stop-loss insurance to protect the trust from exposure to major claims, specific and aggregate.

Not long after these reassuring words were written, Gorman would claim in court that IPCMEA Trust and its trustees (the individuals with "many years of experience in the administration and management of union health and welfare funds") had ripped off Alliance members for over $900,000 in unpaid medical claims.

In August 1996, the U.S. Department of Labor filed a suit in a Chicago federal court seeking a temporary restraining order against IPCMEU, its principals, and related organizations.[25]

In October, the federal judge hearing the case ordered the unions and their trust funds to be liquidated and named an independent fiduciary to oversee the liquidation. In its suit, the Department of Labor accused the union's trustees of misappropriating funds for their own personal use. These funds were used, they claimed, to pay trustees' bills for personal cellular phones, furniture rental, vitamins, health club memberships, car repairs, an $11,000 dental bill, and a $2,500 treadmill exercise machine (charged to one trustee's health insurance). The suit also alleged that in July 1996, as IPCMEU was collapsing, the trustees siphoned money and other items out of the union by authorizing "severance pay" of $20,000 to two of the trustees, giving away the furniture from the union's offices to employees, and giving away the union's expensive computer equipment to a computer consulting firm.

According to the independent fiduciary's analysis, by the end of 1996, the IPCMEA Trust had assets of approximately $500,000 and liabilities of approximately $5 million for a shortfall of $4.5 million. Just over $3 million of those liabilities represented the costs of unpaid medical claims.[26]

The central argument of the Department of Labor's civil suit against IPCMEU and its offshoot unions was that "the primary reason for the creation of these entities was an attempt to evade state regulation as an unlicensed insurance company by the respective states in which the health benefits were being marketed."[27] They were not legitimate unions. Lawyers for IPCMEU claimed that it was indeed a legitimate labor organization and produced evidence showing that the Illinois Department of Labor and the National Labor Relations Board had officially recognized the union as the representative of employees at two Chicago companies.[28] These two firms, however, had a total of only eight employees, whereas IPCMEU provided health insurance to over 4,000 employees nationwide. But the question remains: What constitutes a legitimate labor organization? Without any certification procedure from the U.S. Department of Labor, the answer remains unclear.

Ironically, the U.S. Department of Labor had begun an audit of IPCMEU in early 1994, two years before they shut the organization down. That audit dragged on throughout the better part of 1995, meaning that during much of IPCMEU's operation, as it took in premiums and failed to pay claims, the purported union was under investigation by the Department of Labor, which did nothing to stop the abuses.

RELIGION OR INSURANCE?

All of the schemes described to this point employ the same basic strategy: (1) create an entity that markets health insurance plans under the guise of being something other than a traditional health insurance company, (2) claim as a result that the entity is exempt from state regulation, (3) operate the plan as a Ponzi scheme, and (4) siphon off premiums until the plan goes bankrupt. A common element in these schemes has been a claim to federal ERISA status as a defense against state regulation. But the same basic strategy can be employed even where ERISA claims are not made. One variant on this theme that has cropped up in a number of states involves putative religious organizations offering what they claim are cooperative arrangements to provide medical care to their members but what insurance regulators claim is simply unlicensed health insurance.

Christian Brotherhood

Texas, with its tradition of conservative politics and fundamentalist churches, has proven to be a fertile ground for insurance scams that use the cover of religion to perpetrate fraud on the faithful. One of the best examples was an organization known as the Christian Brotherhood, originally the National Protestant Brotherhood. The organization was founded in 1963 by a group of business and civic leaders in Austin who designed it to serve the needs of the local African American community. The National Protestant Brotherhood was chartered as a fraternal benefit society, which under Texas law allowed it to offer its members health insurance without conforming to the regulatory requirements imposed on licensed insurance companies. In the mid-1980s a local businessman named Bob Rogers gained control of it, changed its name to the Christian Brotherhood, and made a number of changes in its orientation. Up to that point the Brotherhood had focused on providing life insurance to a relatively small group of church members. Under Rogers, the organization embarked on an aggressive telemarketing campaign to sell health insurance to anyone "of good moral character who is a member of, or affiliated with a Baptist, Catholic, Christian, Evangelical or Protestant church or church organization" or was a member of a nonprofit charitable or benevolent organization.[29] The campaign primarily targeted the elderly.

The sales program was a smashing success. By 1987, the organization was bringing in between $5 and $6 million a year in premiums. But at the same time, the Brotherhood had caught the attention of state insurance regulators; they had begun to receive complaints about the organization and its agents' high-pressure sales tactics, used to coax the elderly into buying insurance policies they didn't need. Insurance regulators were also concerned about the extravagant salaries paid to a number of people who worked for the organization. Despite the fact that it was supposedly a nonprofit, fraternal benefit society, its head, Rogers, was being paid $200,000 a year, and some of its agents were making in excess of $100,000. Also on the Brotherhood's payroll was Rogers's wife and several of his other relatives who, together, were being paid between $300,000 and $400,000.[30]

In June 1988, the Texas Board of Insurance seized control of the Christian Brotherhood and all of its assets, calling the group a "peril to the public."[31] Eventually, regulators would determine that the Brotherhood's mismanagement (if not outright fraud) had left some 1,200 policyholders with $1.2 million in unpaid medical claims.[32]

One might think that such a turn of events would have put a damper on Rogers's insurance career or at least forced him to move to a faraway state to start anew. Not so. In 1994, just six years after Christian Brotherhood was shut down, Bob Rogers reappeared in the public spotlight, this time as a candidate for, of all things, insurance commissioner of Oklahoma. Rogers had come out of nowhere to win enough votes in a primary election to enter a runoff election to be the Democratic candidate for the position. Rogers was viewed as a serious contender for the post by his opponent, Carroll Fisher, until the Fisher camp learned of his earlier Texas troubles; they also learned that in 1993 the Oklahoma Department of Insurance had revoked his insurance license for pocketing premiums.[33] Fisher quickly made this information part of the campaign, and she beat Rogers in the runoff election by a three-to-one margin. After his defeat, Rogers claimed that he was the victim of a conspiracy among large insurance companies and insurance regulators.[34]

The All Saints Program

In 1991, the All Saints Program (ASP) was created by Jack Prater in the east Texas town of Tyler. Prater previously had run a similar plan under the name the Golden Rule Program. Prater and his associates advertised their plan in periodicals such as the *Baptist Standard* and the *Bible Baptist Tribune*. In their brochures, ASP officials described the structure of the program:

The ASP is a fellowship of like-minded Christians sharing medical expenses. . . . You, with all your fellow members, will be sharing needs up to $25,000. Those over $25,000 are covered up to $1,000,000 by a group policy issued from the United States Life Insurance company . . . , an A+ rated carrier.

The program revolves around the Monthly Newsletter. The Newsletter is published on the 10th of each month and contains the names of those with medical expense needs, a brief description of the medical problem, cause and the Total Family Single Share

Amount. . . . Send in your share by the 25th of the month. The Administrative Office . . . will disburse, in one check, the share need to those named. Total Month's Share is determined by dividing all on-hand needs requests by the number of eligible families plus the monthly dues amount. . . . The average monthly share for 1993 was less than $122 per family ($61 for single family members). The largest Family Monthly Share to date has been $149.

The brochure adamantly declared that ASP "IS NOT AN INSURANCE PLAN" and its authors were careful not to use terms like "premiums" but instead referred to members' contributions as "shares."

In April 1995, state regulators in Texas obtained a cease and desist order against All Saints, claiming that the organization was simply selling unlicensed insurance. By the time it was shut down, ASP had some 5,000 members. Regulators claimed that Jack Prater and his wife Patsy diverted some $400,000 from the fund for their own personal use over an 18-month period.[35] Among the Praters' victims was a young couple whose daughter was born with a severe birth defect that led to her death three weeks after she was born. While still mourning their child's death, the parents learned that their names had disappeared from the "persons with needs list" published in the ASP newsletter and that they would be hit with over $60,000 in medical bills.[36]

MUTUAL CARE MINISTRIES

The All Saints Program was just one of a number of so-called mutual care ministries that began emerging in the 1980s offering what were referred to as *medical sharing plans* to their members. All operate via subscriptions to "newsletters" in which participants' "medical needs" are paid for through voluntary contributions. The largest and probably best known of these is the Christian Brotherhood Newsletter (CBN).[37] The organization was founded in 1982 by Rev. Bruce Hawthorne of Barberton, Ohio, and grew steadily so that by 1996 it provided medical coverage to some 80,000 subscribers all over the country.[38]

The plan works in the following way. Individuals and their families apply for membership in the program by completing a prequalification form that asks questions about family medical history and requires the applicant to sign a statement that reads:

I attest that the participating adult members of my family are Christians by Biblical principles, and that all subscribing members of my family attend Church regularly (3 out of 4 weeks, weather and health permitting) and totally abstain from alcohol, tobacco, illegal drugs and a homosexual lifestyle.[39]

After being accepted into the program, each family or individual sends to the CBN a monthly fee ranging from $25 to $300. With a membership of some 25,000 families, in 1993 the CBN was receiving $2.7 million a month in contributions.[40]

Eleven months out of the year, family subscribers receive a computer-generated postcard that describes the "medical needs" of another subscriber. The recipient of the postcard is expected to pay a predetermined proportion of the listed person's medical bills. The individual with the "need" receives a list of individuals to whom the postcard has been mailed and is asked to contact CBN headquarters if money is not received. The CBN plan is very restrictive about the "needs" it will cover. Not included are any preexisting condition, the first $200 of any medical bill, routine doctor visits and prescriptions, psychological counseling, dental or eye services.[41]

In its literature, the CBN is very careful to distinguish its plan from insurance:

The Christian Brotherhood Newsletter is a publication, giving subscribers an opportunity to practice New Testament principles by praying for, sending letters of encouragement to, and voluntarily contributing to other subscribers' medical expenses. It is not, and should never be considered or referred to as an insurance company.[42]

Insurance regulators in a number of states have disagreed. To them the plan is simply unlicensed health insurance. The CBN was banned in Delaware in 1993. A regulator there characterized the program as "insurance with a wink" and a "pyramid scheme" that was destined to fail.[43] The same regulator was quoted as saying, "These guys are not bad guys, they just don't know what they're doing."[44] According to a Kentucky insurance regulator, by the spring of 1994, the CBN plan was $3 million behind in its payments to subscribers.[45]

Throughout the early 1990s, the CBN battled with insurance regulators in a number of states. In most of these battles they emerged victorious. A number of states—including Kentucky, Maryland, Minnesota, Oklahoma, Pennsylvania, and Washington—passed special legislation recognizing CBN as a noninsurance carrier with the right to operate outside of state regulation.

Insurance regulators claim that CBN and other mutual care ministries are not necessarily involved in criminal enterprises but nevertheless put their members at risk, with no guarantee that their medical bills will be paid. Regulators also claim that CBN's membership requirements, by excluding gays and non-Christians, are discriminatory. CBN's head, Reverend Hawthorne, responded to that criticism by arguing, "the insurance industry is based on discrimination. You get three speeding tickets and you'll understand that." As for people who don't meet their membership requirements, "let them start a plan like ours."[46]

The CBN is the largest of at least half a dozen similarly structured mutual care ministries operating across the United States, including the Christian Care Medi-Share Program, Samaritan Ministries International, and the Good Samaritan Program. In their literature, all of these organizations make it clear that they do not consider themselves to be selling insurance. Yet their program descriptions sound very much like health insurance plans, with some referring to "deductibles" and "preexisting conditions." The Good Samaritan Program of Beech Grove, Indiana, even has a stop-loss policy with an insurance company to cover "needs" in excess of $25,000.[47] At what point they cross the line and become unlicensed health insurers is a matter of ongoing debate and litigation.

CONCLUSIONS

This chapter has examined a wide range of organizations, from phony labor unions to religiously based mutual benefit societies. These groups all offer their members some type of medical benefits while steadfastly denying that they are in the business of selling insurance. In many ways they represent a return to the origins of health insurance in the mutual benefit societies of the nineteenth century, in which individuals with a common bond would contribute to funds that provided benefits to workers who lost income due to accident or illness. These earlier associations generally worked because they operated locally and their participants knew each other. In contemporary societies, where these organizations can easily operate nationally and internationally, such bonds are absent and members are more vulnerable to fraud. Under these conditions, government agencies have felt an obligation to intervene to protect the interests of citizens. At the same time, the inability or unwillingness of these government agencies to precisely define entities such as labor unions, mutual benefit societies, and insurance companies has led to the kinds of problems and issues raised here.

One of the reasons these groups have prospered is economic. They provide medical coverage to consumers at significantly lower prices than do commercial insurance companies. In many cases, of course, this is because their operators never intend to pay claims.

Another explanation for these groups' appeal is their skillful use of populist rhetoric. In their literature and sales pitches, the promoters of these plans express a disdain for both government bureaucrats and large insurance companies, both of whom are portrayed as squeezing the "little guy." After Bob Rogers, the former head of the Christian Brotherhood, lost in his bid to become Oklahoma's insurance commissioner, he told the press:

I am like David against Goliath and the army of Philistines. I only have five smooth stones in the slingshot. Goliath (the insurance commissioner) has an army of high-paid lawyers and hundreds of employees to do her every bidding and millions of tax dollars at her disposal.[48]

Similar David versus Goliath themes also appeared in the public statements and promotional literature of Lawernce Kenemore and his Association of Trust and Guarantee. Soon after state regulators seized control of ATG's offices in southern California, Kenemore issued the following communique to his clients:

Tuesday Sept. 7, 1993, California Department of Insurance, on be-half of the vested interests (i.e. insurance companies and agents and workers' comp. lawyers), illegally seized the ATG offices in Fountain Valley. Larry Kenemore, Senior partner of ATG and his staff were thrown out of the offices into the parking lot. The State Insurance Commissioner's lackeys started manning the phones and misinforming ATG clients.[49]

Such statements undoubtedly hold a certain appeal to many small business owners and employees who have been virtually abandoned by large insurance companies. For them, a conspiracy between the insurance industry and government regulators may not seem all that implausible. This sentiment was expressed by one subscriber to the Christian Brotherhood Newsletter:

Insurance companies for the most part are 80 percent crooked. [With CBN] we know where our money is going. We know what our money is doing.[50]

The public's distrust of insurance companies and big business in general is reflected in public opinion polls. A Gallup Poll conducted in 1995 asked respondents to rank the honesty and ethical standards of people in 25 occupations. Insurance salespeople came in 21st, just above car salespeople, advertisers, and members of Congress.[51]

Still another reason for these groups' success in persuading people to hand over their hard-earned cash in exchange for nothing more tangible than a promise lies in their ability to convince their prospective clients that they are participating in something that transcends a mere economic transaction. By making their contributions, participants are told, they are not simply ensuring that their medical needs will be met but are also advancing the goals of a group or a cause in which they firmly believe. Participants in these schemes are willing to suspend the normal precautions they exercise when in engaging in business transactions because they trust the health plan's promoters and desire to help others with whom they share a spiritual, philosophical, or ethnic tie. Some law enforcement officials have begun referring to these scams as *affinity group fraud* to describe the affinity felt by the participants toward each other.[52]

One of the best examples of affinity group fraud is found in a case that revolved around a wealthy Seattle businessman named Philip Harmon. In the fall of 1997, Harmon pleaded guilty to federal charges alleging that he perpetrated a health insurance scam that left some 6,500 persons, many of whom were members of the Quaker church, with unpaid medical claims. Harmon, his son, and his son-in-law operated two health insurance trusts that were intended to cover the medical expenses of Quaker ministers and others around the country. In February 1997, insurance regulators claimed the trusts were on the verge of collapse and moved to shut them down. Harmon also bilked church members, many of whom were elderly, out of money they had given him to invest. Through these two schemes, prosecutors estimated, Harmon and his associates swindled investors and health care customers out of as much as $40 million. As testimony to the role that belief and trust play in these schemes, many of Harmon's victims expressed faith in his honesty, even after losing money to him. One investor who lost $200,000 in Harmon's investment schemes was quoted as saying, "He is trying to do what is right. I really believe that." [53]

NOTES

1 Michael Flagg, "State Gets Control of Insurance Agency," *Los Angeles Times,* 31 March 1993, p. D-6.

2 *Insurance Commissioner v. Bestland Insurance Agency,* No. 707–884 (Super. Ct., Orange County, California 1993).

3 *In the matter of People's Assurance Cooperative,* Order to Cease and Desist. File no. LA 14206-AP. 1992.

4 *In the matter of People's Assurance Cooperative,* note 3 *supra,* 4. It is not uncommon for bogus offshore insurers to claim assets whose value is difficult if not impossible to assess. In one case, the operator of a bogus firm even fabricated where the company was located.

In 1996, a federal grand jury in Dallas indicted Jeffrey H. Reynolds, the president of an offshore company known as California Pacific Bankers & Insurance Ltd. Reynolds claimed that the company was based in a fictitious country known as the "Dominion of Melchizedek," which he variously indicated was located either west of Antarctica or off the coast of Colombia. Reynolds also claimed that the "Dominion" maintained an embassy in Washington, D.C. Curiously, premium checks were mailed to the company at an address in Dallas. *United States v. Reynolds,* No. 96-CR-0003 (N.D. Tex. 1996).

5 *California v. Kenemore,* No. A-391659 (Super. Ct., Los Angeles County, California 1983).

6 *IAEA v. Kenemore,* No. 92–09078 (101st Judicial Dist., Dallas County, Texas 1992).

7 *Insurance Commissioner v. Bestland,* note 2 *supra,* 6, "Complaint."

8 *Reich v. Kenemore,* No. 3-95-CV-0105-R (N.D. Tex. 1995).

9 Missouri Department of Insurance, news release, 12 October 1993, as quoted in *Central Health Corp. v. Kenemore,* No. 94-CV-5016 (W.D. Ark. 1994).

10 Frank Doolittle, "ATG Case Study," *NAIC Special Report,* May/June 1995, p. 8.

11 *Reich v. Kenemore,* note 8 *supra.*

12 *United States v. Kenemore*, No. 3-95-CR-099-D (N.D. Tex. 1995).

13 Doolittle, "ATG Case Study," 8.

14 *Central Health Corp. v. Kenemore*, note 9 *supra*.

15 Mary Lee Johnson is a pseudonym.

16 *Reich v. Kenemore*, note 8 *supra*.

17 James Brook, "Officials Say Montana 'Freemen' Collected $1.8 Million in Scheme," *New York Times*, 29 March 1996, p. A1.

18 Barry Meier, "The Lien King on the Attack," *New York Times*, 29 June 1995, p. D1. A California disciple of the Montana Freemen, who had anointed herself the "lien queen," was sentenced to 17 years in prison after she issued checks that were backed by liens against the U.S. government totaling $1 billion. Brad Knickerbocker, "New Militia Tactic: Paper Terrorism," *Christian Science Monitor*, 15 October 1997, p. 1.

19 Tom Laceky, "Courts Befuddled by 'Freemanspeak,'" *Burlington Free Press*, 26 October 1997, p. 6A.

20 *United States v. Kenemore*, note 12 *supra*, Judicial Notice of Status Pursuant Texas Rules 52.

21 Bill Lodge, "Judge Frees Arlington Man Pending Trial in Benefits Theft," *Dallas Morning News*, 8 April 1995, p. 39A.

22 Ibid.

23 Bill Lodge, "Wife Gets 5 Months in Insurance Scheme." *Dallas Morning News*, 7 October 1996, p. 1A.

24 Chris Petrakos, "Taking Root: More Insurers Find Alternative Medicine Grows on Them," *Chicago Tribune*, 2 August 1995, p. C1; Janet Firshein, "Picture Alternative Medicine in the Mainstream," *Business and Health*, 1 April 1995, p. 28.

25 *Metzler v. Wolfe*, No. 96-C-4801 (N.D. Ill. 1996).

26 *Metzler v. Wolfe*, note 25 *supra*, "Independent Fiduciary's Third Progress Report."

27 *Metzler v. Wolfe*, note 25 *supra*, 15, "First Amended Complaint."

28 *Metzler v. Wolfe*, note 25 *supra*, documents.

29 John Kirkpatrick, "State Probes Fast-Growing Insurance Firm's Practices," *Dallas Morning News*, 24 December 1987, p. 1A.

30 Ibid.

31 John Kirkpatrick, "Insurance Firm Under State Rule," *Dallas Morning News*, 30 June 1988, p. 33A.

32 John Kirkpatrick, "Oklahoma Candidate Had Texas Troubles," *Dallas Morning News*, 24 September 1994, p. 1A.

33 Ibid.

34 Brian Ford, "Democrat Fisher Bests Rogers in Insurance Race," *Tulsa World,* 21 September 1994, p. N8.

35 "State Shuts Down Christian Medical-Expense Program," *Dallas Morning News,* 18 May 1995, p. 12D.

36 Unpublished documents, Texas Department of Insurance (n.d.).

37 The Christian Brotherhood Newsletter has no connection to Roger's Christian Brotherhood discussed earlier.

38 Laura Klepacki, "A Little Charity Can Cover a Lot of Bills," *Star-Ledger* (Newark), 2 January 1997, p. 41.

39 Christian Brotherhood Newsletter, "Fact Pak" (Akron: n.p., n.d.).

40 Joyce Price, "Paying Medical Bills on Faith," *Washington Times,* 25 December 1993, p. A5.

41 Ibid., 4.

42 "Fact Pak," 6.

43 Price, "Paying Medical Bills."

44 Michael deCourcy Hinds, "Christian Group Criticized As Unsound Insurance Plan," *New York Times,* 14 June 1994, p. A10.

45 Kristen Svingen, "Insured Christians Trust God—And Each Other," *Charleston Gazette,* 15 March 1994, p. 1C.

46 Ibid.

47 Untitled pamphlet published by the Good Samaritan Program, Beech Grove, Indiana.

48 Arnold Hamilton, "Oklahoma Hopeful Discusses Troubled Past," *Dallas Morning News,* 10 September 1994, p. 29A.

49 Letter from Lawernce Kenemore to ATG clients (n.d.).

50 Svingen, "Insured Christians Trust God."

51 U.S. Department of Justice, Bureau of Justice Statistics, *Sourcebook of Criminal Justice Statistics, 1995,* (Washington, D.C.: GPO, 1996), Table 2.16, p. 138.

52 Michael Paulson, "Swindlers Showing an Affinity to Rip Off Their Own," *Seattle Post-Intelligencer,* 13 November 1997, p. A-4.

53 Scott Sundee, "Investors Face Loss of Their Nest Eggs," *Seattle Post-Intelligencer,* 2 February 1997, p. A-1.

The Political Economy of Reform

CHAPTER SIX

THE preceding chapters have shown how insurance con artists have used the loopholes in federal laws to set up phony health insurance plans that have defrauded hundreds of thousands of Americans out of millions of dollars. Given that these opportunities for fraud were created by federal legislation, the solution would seem obvious: Change the laws! This was exactly the conclusion that several congressional panels reached after studying the problem in the late 1980s and early 1990s. Yet despite the consistent support of groups like the National Association of Insurance Commissioners and the National Governors Association, these changes to the Employee Retirement Income Security Act (ERISA) were never made. Individual states, with legal authority granted by the courts, were forced to take the initiative and to enact piecemeal legislation that gave them greater authority over multiple employer welfare arrangements (MEWAS) and other ERISA health plans. But in the face of federal inaction on ERISA reform, the states' uneven efforts resulted in only a limited ability to control fraudulent schemes.

The failure of Congress to deal with the regulatory loopholes created by ERISA did not result from successful lobbying efforts by the insurance crooks themselves (although in some instances, crooked MEWA owners such as Edward Zinner did testify before Congress [see Chapter 2]). Rather, this congressional inaction reflected the considerable political clout wielded by powerful interest groups that saw efforts to change ERISA as an attack on a system that provided them substantial financial benefits, benefits they fought very hard to preserve.

The stories told in the last few chapters focused on unscrupulous individuals and their individual criminal schemes. At this point the story must shift to the broader landscape of organized economic and political groups that exert a powerful influence over the regulatory laws promulgated in Washington and over the manner in which they are enforced across the country. In other words, we must now consider the broader political economy that creates the structural opportunities for white-collar crime in the small business health insurance industry.

The story is not one of payoffs, bribes, and influence peddling among corrupt politicians. It is a much more mundane one of how well-organized interest groups legally pursued their interests and in doing so stymied the efforts of regulators to clamp down on illegal health insurance scams. While perhaps making for less exciting reading than Watergate-like tales of secret meetings and code-named informants, it is probably a story that more accurately reflects the ordinary way in which federal regulatory laws are formulated.

Regulatory laws, such as those that govern the insurance industry, are often such arcane topics that the mainstream press rarely reports on them. Consequently, the public rarely learns about technical changes in regulations that might be mind-numbing to read but that may have an enormous influence on their lives. In the early 1980s, for example, when Congress passed a series of laws deregulating the thrift industry, laws that effectively paved the way for the most costly set of white-collar crimes in U.S. history, these events went almost unreported in the national media. And so it is with health insurance regulations. Of the millions of Americans who receive essential health care through ERISA plans, it is doubtful that more than a small percentage have ever even heard the term *ERISA*. By contrast, benefits experts within large corporations, labor unions, and trade associations are intimately familiar with the densely worded provisions of ERISA because they know that even slight changes to the law may cost their organizations millions of dollars. And when those changes are proposed, lobbyists are swiftly dispatched to the corridors of Washington where they ply their craft, attempting to dissuade lawmakers from modifying the regulations from which their clients have benefited so greatly.

THE POLITICS OF ERISA

In 1974, when Congress was debating the "mysteries of ERISA," the discussions were long and tedious, eventually comprising several thousand pages in the *Congressional Record*. Only five of those pages were about the health care provisions in the bill.[1] Despite this lack of discussion on the House and Senate floors, the preemption clause that exempted employee benefit plans from state regulation was the subject of lobbying by several powerful groups, notably organized labor, which was "eager to prevent the states from taxing and regulating the health and pension plans they had negotiated under the Taft-Hartley Act."[2] Amazingly, given the tremendous impact the ERISA provisions would have on the health insurance industry, representatives of the industry were largely silent on the bill. As one high official in the Blue Cross Association put it, "very little was going on because nobody saw it; nobody in the health insurance industry understood the implication of the preemption."[3] Many other groups that would be affected greatly by the law, including large corporations and state insurance regulators, were also seemingly unaware of its significance.

By the late 1980s, however, as problems in the MEWA industry were reaching serious levels, many of these groups were expressing grave concerns about ERISA's consequences. Having recently dealt with scams like Rubell-Helm (see Chapter 2) and Cap Staffing (see Chapter 3), frustrated state regulators were appearing before congressional panels with tales of egregious fraud and lame responses by the Department of Labor, which in theory was monitoring these programs. In 1989, the deputy commissioner of Washington state's insurance commission told the House Subcommittee on Retirement Income and Employment about her frustrated attempts to persuade the U.S. Department of Labor to take action against fraudulent MEWA operators in that state. She cited as an example a series of interactions between her office and the Department of Labor that began in February 1989 when she informed the Department's Pension and Welfare Benefits Administration (PWBA), the agency with specific jurisdiction over ERISA plans, of several fraudulent MEWAs operating in the Northwest. She identified one such MEWA as Northwest Loggers Association, run by a Gary Stone.

I made it understood that substantial harm to hundreds of consumers who relied on this health care coverage was imminent. . . . PWBA advised me that they already knew about the problems with Northwest Loggers and Mr. Stone yet had taken no action.

Although . . . I was promised action on the part of PWBA, no action or assistance at all was forthcoming. I waited approximately three months. During calls I made to PWBA during this waiting period, the original offers of help became less promising. I was advised by PWBA that its Seattle Regional Office had few employees and handles five states. I was further advised that PWBA Seattle employees have expertise in pension plans and not in ERISA health care arrangements such as MEWAs and that it simply does not have the priority or resources to adequately handle MEWA problems.

By the time Northwest Loggers received its Cease and Desist order, it was already insolvent. Mr. Stone immediately departed the state, taking with him an undetermined amount of Northwest Loggers' funds. He also left hundreds of consumers in some six states with thousands—probably hundreds of thousands—of dollars of unpaid medical claims and with no medical coverage. To date I know of no criminal, civil or other disciplinary action taken or

planned by any division of DOL or any other entity. I am advised
that Mr. Stone has now settled in Nevada, where he is setting up
another alleged MEWA.[4]

Similar frustrations were expressed in 1990 by Texas insurance regulators when they appeared before Senator Nunn's
committee. Describing MEWAS as "ticking time bombs" that
had already cost Texas residents over $19 million, and ERISA
as a "regulatory black hole" that had severely limited the
states' ability to deal with fraudulent health plans, the regulators offered a withering criticism of PWBA:

State regulators . . . sometimes must ask the Department of Labor's
Pension and Welfare Benefits Administration (PWBA) for opinions
on whether specific plans qualify for the ERISA preemption of state
regulatory authority. Commonly, however, PWBA never has heard
of a particular plan and has no record of its existence. Documentation may not be on file at the Department of Labor (if at all) until
months after a plan has gone into business and has begun collecting
contributions. When documentation is present, the DOL's record of
openly and swiftly sharing information with concerned states has
been poor.[5]

Even officials at the Department of Labor blasted PWBA's
poor performance in policing ERISA plans. In 1989, Raymond
Maria, the Department of Labor's Inspector General, told a
congressional panel:

The failure of the Department of Labor to conceptualize and maintain a strong and integrated enforcement strategy has created a window of opportunity for those who would embezzle and steal from
plan participants.[6]

Maria went further, suggesting that the Department's tepid response was the result of more than bureaucratic ineptitude:

Unfortunately, our [the Office of the Inspector General] efforts with
regard to employee benefit plans have almost always been met with
resistance from the Department of Labor, which appears to defer

more to the voices of industry rather than the voices of plan participants.[7]

Not only was PWBA failing to effectively respond to the growing problems of MEWA fraud, its officials had no idea how many MEWAS—legitimate or illegitimate—were out there, a fact that PWBA's head, George Ball, reluctantly admitted to Senator Nunn in 1990 hearings:

SENATOR NUNN: So, basically, you are saying, Mr. Ball, that you really cannot tell us this morning how many Americans out there, men and women who believe they are insured, really do not have any insurance, because the companies they are involved in are not even known to the Department of Labor or to the States, and many of them are not going to know the problems until the claims simply cannot be paid. Is that what you are saying?

MR. BALL: Yes, sir, I am saying that neither we nor anyone else has an accurate picture of the scope of the MEWA problem.[8]

The complaints made by state regulators were affirmed in March 1992 when the General Accounting Office (GAO) released its study of MEWA fraud. Based on a survey of state insurance departments, the GAO estimated that "between January 1988 and June 1991, MEWAS left at least 398,000 participants and their beneficiaries with over $123 million in unpaid claims and many other participants without insurance."[9] The results of the GAO study were widely reported in newspapers around the country, and for a brief moment the problem was part of a broader discussion about deficiencies in the nation's health care system.

Responding to these criticisms, in 1992 members of Congress sponsored no less than four bills that sought to clarify the regulatory status of ERISA health plans. Three of those bills, sponsored by Republicans, would have maintained federal (Department of Labor) oversight over MEWAS and other ERISA plans, although with varying requirements for financial conditions and reporting.[10] The fourth, a bill sponsored by

Senator Nunn, would have essentially shifted all regulatory authority over these plans to individual states and would have allowed them to impose considerably stricter requirements than were found in the other bills.[11]

In the debates over these pieces of proposed legislation, the battle lines and interests of the affected parties emerged. On one side were Senator Nunn and the state insurance commissioners who favored shifting all regulatory authority over MEWAS to the states, which would then be allowed to impose all the standards on MEWAS that they did on insurance companies. On the other side of the debate was a coalition consisting of the MEWA industry itself, representatives of big business, and the Bush administration. For varying reasons, all of these groups wanted the Department of Labor, rather than the individual states, to maintain regulatory authority over ERISA plans.

Representing the interests of large companies that self-insure, the Self-Insurance Institute of America expressed concern that "the current problems associated with MEWAS could reflect unfavorably on financially sound, bona fide, self-funded MEWAS as well as many sound, single-employer self-funded health benefit plans."[12] The AFL-CIO supported the idea of putting MEWAS under state regulation but held firm to the idea "that collectively bargained multi-employer welfare plans are to be treated like all other ERISA plans and not to be treated as MEWAS."[13]

In the end, none of the measures passed. When the 102d Congress came to a close, the ambiguities and loopholes in ERISA that had allowed insurance swindlers to steal millions of dollars remained in place.

THE STATES ACT

Frustrated by inaction in Washington while they watched their residents being ripped off by insurance crooks, in the early 1990s a number of states enacted their own laws, extending their jurisdiction over MEWAs and health plans offered by employee leasing companies. The states paved the way for these legislative measures by winning key victories in the courts.

In *MDPhysicians v. Wrotenberry,* a federal district court ruled that while a health plan may constitute a MEWA, it may not meet the standards under ERISA of an "employee benefit plan." In that case, MDPhysicians was an organization marketing health plans as a self-funded MEWA to employers in Texas. The state sought regulatory authority over the organization as a health insurer. The court ruled that MDPhysicians was a MEWA but was not an "employee benefit plan" as envisioned by ERISA because it did not act "directly as an employer or indirectly in the interest of an employer" and was therefore subject to state regulation.[14] In a Connecticut case, *Atlantic Healthcare Benefits Trust v. Goggins,* the Connecticut Department of Insurance argued that Atlantic was not an ERISA-qualified MEWA and therefore required a certificate of authority to do business in that state as a licensed insurer. The owners of Atlantic (Edward Zinner et al.; see Chapter 2) contended that the plan was a qualified MEWA and therefore was exempt from state regulation. The court of appeals ruled that, according to ERISA, as a self-funded MEWA Atlantic was subject to state regulations, and that states were within their rights to require MEWAs to obtain certificates of authority.[15] With these rulings behind them, a number of states moved quickly to pass legislation clarifying their regulatory authority over MEWAS.

Even before these rulings, the states were on the move. In 1991, the Florida legislature enacted a law that required all self-insured MEWAs to obtain certificates of authority from the state Department of Insurance. To obtain those certificates, MEWAS are required to maintain surplus requirements of 10 percent of liabilities and file annual reports with the department.[16] Many MEWAs had difficulty meeting these requirements. By the spring of 1994, only 4 of the 28 MEWAS originally issued certificates remained active.[17]

A similar law requiring MEWA licensing was enacted in

Texas in 1993. That law required entities meeting the federal definition of a self-insured or partially insured MEWA to obtain a certificate from the state Department of Insurance every year.[18] By the spring of 1997, only 12 MEWAS were licensed to do business in Texas.[19] Nationwide, by 1997, about half the states required self-insured MEWAS to obtain a certificate of authority or a license before doing business.[20]

In addition to keeping closer tabs on MEWAS, state insurance regulators wanted the legal authority to regulate employee leasing firms that sold health insurance to their clients. The courts and the U.S. Department of Labor made that task easier. In *Texas v. Alliance Employee Leasing Corporation*, a federal court in the Northern District of Texas determined that Alliance was not a valid employee welfare benefit plan because it did not constitute an employer under the definition used by ERISA.[21] The Department of Labor, in a series of formal opinions, clarified the regulatory status of employee leasing firms under ERISA. These opinions generally held that employee leasing firms did not meet the requirements for a single employer but did constitute MEWAS; they therefore would be subject to state regulation to the extent provided under ERISA.[22]

The states quickly responded to these developments by enacting regulatory legislation. In 1991, Florida enacted the first law requiring employee leasing firms to obtain a license from the state. Those regulations also prohibited employee leasing firms from self-insuring health plans.[23] In 1993, the Texas legislature passed a bill that required all employee leasing firms operating in the state to obtain a license from the state Department of Licensing and Regulation. One of the licensing requirements was that leasing firms maintain a minimum amount of assets ranging from $50,000 to $100,000, depending on the company's size.[24] All leasing firms were required to be licensed by March 1, 1994. By April of that year, only 110 of an estimated 250 to 300 firms doing business in the state had met the requirement.[25] By April 1997, that number had increased to 160.[26]

As the states took positive steps to protect consumers by

enacting more stringent regulatory laws, forces were organizing in Washington to press for legislation that would reverse the states' gains by once again deregulating MEWAS.

STEPPING BACKWARD

The congressional elections of 1994 swept into office a number of conservative Republicans who, under the leadership of House Speaker Newt Gingrich, declared a "Republican Revolution" in American politics. Foremost among their ideological principles was a belief in the sovereignty of the free market and a disdain for federal intervention in the economy. To some of the soldiers in the new conservative revolution, the efforts of state officials to regulate small business people who were banding together to reduce their health insurance rates smacked of the very kind of heavy-handed, governmental interference in the marketplace that they so opposed. To them, MEWAS and other types of private alliances among businesses formed to promote the interests of employees were exactly the kinds of organizations that should be encouraged, rather than discouraged by onerous, bureaucratic red tape.

A year earlier, the Clinton administration had included in its health care reform package provisions that would have encouraged the formation of health insurance "purchasing alliances"—state-regulated and -monitored organizations that would have pooled the resources of small businesses to purchase health insurance. House Republicans opposed the purchasing alliance concept precisely *because* it called for governmental oversight. From their perspective, this was just governmental control over free enterprise dressed up in different clothing.

In the 104th session of Congress, House Republicans, led by Rep. Harris Fawell of Illinois, proposed legislation that would have allowed MEWAS and employee leasing companies to apply to the Department of Labor for an exemption from state regulations.[27] Critics claimed that the bill was simply an attempt to overturn state regulation in favor of a return to the bad old days in which MEWAS and employee leasing companies were free to hide behind ERISA's preemption clause to perpetrate frauds. Despite strong support from small business groups like the National Federation of Independent Business (NFIB) and from representatives of large corporations such as the National Association of Manufacturers (NAM) the bill was not enacted into law.[28]

The next year, 1996, Congressman Fawell sponsored similar legislation that would have allowed MEWAS to opt out of state regulation in favor of Department of Labor oversight. State and health insurance industry leaders strongly opposed the bill, concerned that it would leave the door wide open for fraud. The National Association of Insurance Commissioners (NAIC) and the National Council of State Legislators warned that "the bill . . . opens up an opportunity for scam operators to operate in a netherworld of loose federal standards with little or no meaningful oversight."[29] Nonetheless, the bill passed the House, and its provisions were attached to the broader Health Insurance Reform Act being considered in the Senate. The act's sponsors Senators Kennedy and Kassebaum were determined to get it enacted into law and stripped it of its controversial elements, including the MEWA provisions.[30]

In 1997 Representative Fawell returned to the floor of the House with a bill (H.R. 1515) that would have allowed small employers to form "association health plans"—for all purposes identical to MEWAS—that could operate free of state regulation. Representative Fawell argued that the legislation would give "small employers precisely the same powers, under ERISA, long enjoyed by corporations such as General Motors."[31] Opponents of the legislation charged that, in addition to opening the door to fraud, the bill (as well as companion legislation introduced in the Senate) would greatly exacerbate existing trends toward cherry picking in the health insurance market by allowing association health plans to create pools of generally healthy individuals who could obtain relatively inexpensive health insurance coverage while abandoning the less healthy to the ranks of the uninsured.[32] Despite these criticisms, Fawell's bill passed in the House and was attached to the budget bill being reviewed by Congress in the summer of 1997. Senate support for the Fawell bill, however, was weak, and when the budget bill was eventually signed by the president on July 30, the association health plan provisions had been dropped.

The preceding discussions on Fawell's legislation show the ideological principles and economic interests that lay behind not only the debate over regulation of ERISA health plans, but also the larger national debate over health care reform. To understand why a straightforward legislative solution to a serious problem in the small business health insurance industry could not be achieved, one has to take a closer look at these ideological and economic factors.

The supporters of Fawell's bills drew on the ideological rhetoric that was current among conservative Republican politicians in Washington, a rhetoric that espoused the virtues of free enterprise unfettered by government regulation and invoked populist imagery of small business owners struggling to compete against all-powerful corporations. These arguments frequently asserted the superiority of the marketplace over governmental control. In supporting Fawell's 1995 bill (H.R. 995), the National Business Coalition in Health, a national employer's group, stated:

To make the market work, it must be protected from the depredations of overzealous regulators who do not believe that it can work. A huge philosophical battle was fought—and lost—last year in the halls of Congress and the court of public opinion by those seeking to replace the market with government control. . . . [H.R. 995] is a welcome counterattack on behalf of market reformers like ourselves.[33]

Another consistent theme found in these arguments was the need to give small businesses a helping hand in their struggles against large corporations and insurance companies. When the editors of the *Washington Post* wrote an editorial questioning the wisdom of exempting MEWAs from state regulation, Representative Fawell responded by implicitly accusing the *Post* editors of hypocrisy and elitism, pointing out that as employees of a large corporation, they were able to enjoy the benefits of a self-insured health plan, exempt from state regulation.[34] "What's good enough for the *Post* is apparently too good for small businesses," Fawell wrote in his own op-ed piece.[35] He went on to note that opposition to his legislation from insurance regulators and insurance companies was predictable.

A few insurance companies that make a living cherry-picking small businesses do not want the competition [a voluntary health association] plan would represent. State insurance commissioners fear that if these associations are successful in covering most small businesses in an essentially free and unregulated market, then they would have nothing to regulate.[36]

Just below the surface of these ideology-laden statements one can see the outline of the economic interests of the parties in the debate. In many ways, the debate over what to do about MEWAs was really a debate over ERISA and the much larger stakes that were involved there. In fact, many of the participants in the MEWA regulation debate had no direct involvement in the MEWA industry, nor did they have any involvement in the small group health insurance market. What they did have was a lot to lose if the ERISA exemptions from state regulation were eliminated or even modified.

THE BIGGER PICTURE:
THE BATTLE OVER ERISA

In the early 1990s, as health care reform efforts stalled in Congress, the states began to take action to initiate health care reform on their own, particularly in the underserved small group segment of the insurance market. According to a GAO report, "between 1990 and 1995 at least 45 states passed legislation that modified the terms and conditions under which insurance is offered to small employers."[37] The substance of these measures varied from state to state, but the broad goals were "to help insure that (1) employees who want health insurance coverage will be accepted and renewed by insurers; (2) waiting periods for preexisting conditions will be short, occur only once, and be based only on recent medical history; (3) coverage will be continuous and portable, even when an individual changes jobs or the employer changes insurers; and (4) extremes in premium costs will be narrowed to fall within ranges specified by the states."[38]

The major obstacle to these state-based efforts was ERISA, and by 1994 state officials were vigorously pleading their case before Congress, asking for waivers to the federal law. The governor of Oregon told a congressional panel that ERISA "blocks the states from being laboratories of change" and had led to an increase in the numbers of the uninsured.[39] The problem was that with so many employees receiving coverage from state-exempt ERISA plans, there were relatively few people who could be affected by state reforms. In the state of Washington, for example, a health care reform package adopted in 1993 requiring insurance companies to sell policies on the basis of a uniform community rate had to be shelved when officials realized that more than half of the state's workforce was covered under ERISA plans and would not be affected by the new policy.[40]

Large corporations and other self-insurers argued just as vigorously against changing ERISA's preemption provisions. The most frequent claim made by these groups was that a change in ERISA would lead to a balkanization of regulatory authority over health plans, thus subjecting large corporate self-insurers to 50 different sets of regulations. Corporate self-insurers also argued that their need to retain flexibility in their health care plans in order to meet the specific needs of their employees would be greatly hindered by state regulations.

The interests of corporate sponsors of ERISA plans were frequently represented in these debates by groups like the ERISA Industry Committee (ERIC), an organization that represents companies with a minimum of 10,000 employees. ERIC's *raison d'être* was the preservation of the ERISA preemption for self-insurance, and its position centered on two arguments: (1) "without ERISA's nationally uniform standards, the most creative, innovative and cost-effective, employer-sponsored health benefit plans could not exist because of the burdens of complying with overlapping and inconsistent state laws"; and (2) differing state regulations "will cause employers and providers to flee from states with more burdensome requirements to states with less burdensome requirements."[41] This position found strong support among a number of influential congressional leaders, including Senate Majority Leader Bob Dole, who told the members of the Self-Insurance Institute of America at their annual meetings in 1995 that Congress "can do many things in health care with no prohibitions on self-insurance."[42]

Looking underneath the surface of these arguments, one quickly sees the real issue in these debates: money. By not being forced to comply with state regulations, large self-insurers save millions of dollars every year, a large portion of which results from the avoidance of state-mandated health benefits. Many states require licensed insurers to provide their policyholders with coverage for a wide range of illnesses, including AIDS and other chronic conditions. By contrast, ERISA plans are generally exempt from these mandated benefits and may deny coverage for illnesses requiring expensive treatments.[43] The financial benefits that corporations reap by avoiding mandates are substantial. One study estimated that mandated benefits increased the cost of health insurance by between 7 and 15 percent.[44] Furthermore, unlike licensed insurance companies, self-funded ERISA plans do not have to pay state premium taxes, which typically range from 2 to 3 percent. For Fortune 100 companies that spend more than $500 million a year on health care benefits, these taxes would add $10 to $15 mil-

lion to their annual costs.[45] Thus, the ERISA preemption from
state regulation saved large companies substantial amounts of
money, and they fought very hard to maintain that privilege.

These issues and interests formed a clearly discernible back-
drop to the debates over the much narrower issue of who
should regulate MEWAS. The linkage between ERISA preemptions for MEWAS and the preemption status of large corporate
self-insured health plans was made clear by groups like NAM.
In their statement supporting Fawell's 1995 legislation, NAM
officials wrote:

[ERISA] has facilitated a private, free market in which nearly 150
million Americans receive health insurance from employers that voluntarily sponsor plans. That's tremendous progress without government mandates. . . . Your bill [H.R. 995] does what needs to be
done: it enables competition and market forces . . . to allow small
employers to band together and improve access to affordable coverage. The NAM believes the problem of smaller employer access
to health coverage can be addressed without disturbing what is
working.[46]

What NAM meant by "what is working" was clear: ERISA. In
fact, NAM's statement went on to argue that ERISA preemption
"should be expanded to eliminate state requirements that insurance products, sold primarily to small businesses, include
state-mandated benefits."[47] ERIC took a similar position in
supporting the 1997 legislation. In a letter to Representative
Fawell regarding H.R. 1515, ERIC's president wrote:

The proposal appears to be consistent with ERIC's general policy
position supporting reduced benefit mandates, enhanced opportunities for group purchasing (especially among small businesses), and
the preservation of ERISA preemption.[48]

As these statements indicate, from the perspective of big
business, moving MEWAS out of state regulatory authority was
a step in the right direction because it affirmed the validity of
the ERISA preemption clause generally. Big business feared
that by allowing states to exert control over one form of ERISA

plans—MEWAS—policy would be put on the slippery slope in which the next step would be to place large self-insurers under state control, where they would be required to provide costly mandated benefits to their employees. Thus, the debate over MEWA regulation was but a skirmish, albeit an important one, in the larger battle over ERISA.

HOW FEDERAL REGULATIONS
ARE NOT MADE

In the debate over MEWA regulation, organized labor remained largely silent. State efforts to regulate MEWAS and employee leasing firms had little effect on labor unions because their health plans remained clearly under ERISA's definitions and thus under federal jurisdiction. Yet by 1994, as federal and state regulators were applying more scrutiny to MEWAS, bogus labor unions had become the vehicle of choice for health insurance scam artists.[49] In Chapter 4 we saw numerous examples of how insurance crooks have used the provisions in ERISA regarding collectively bargained employee benefit plans to sell worthless insurance policies to thousands of unwitting victims. The operators of these schemes knew that they could run their scams for a year or two (plenty of time to steal millions of dollars) before being shut down because of the inability of federal authorities to determine if their organization was a bona fide labor union.

To fill this gap in the law, in August 1995, the Department of Labor proposed a new set of regulations that would define what constituted an "employee labor organization" as well as provide a definition of ERISA employee benefit plans "established pursuant to a collective bargaining plan."[50] Health plans that did not meet these criteria would be regarded as MEWAS and therefore subject to state regulation to the extent allowed by ERISA. Plans that met the criteria would be regarded as bona fide ERISA plans and would be exempt from state regulation. The proposed regulations were clearly designed to prevent people like Lawernce Kenemore and his Association of Trust and Guarantee and William Loeb and his Consolidated Local 867 from marketing health insurance under the guise of being a labor union. The regulations stated that to be considered an employee labor organization, an organization "must operate for a substantial purpose other than that of offering or providing health coverage" and may not utilize "the services of licensed insurance agents or brokers for soliciting employers or participants in connection with a collectively bargained plan."[51] Furthermore, in a clear effort to eliminate the abuses resulting from the enrollment of "associate members" in union health plans, the regulations stated that "a plan will not be considered to be established or maintained pursuant to one or more collective bargaining agreements unless no less than 85 percent of the individuals covered by the plan are present or certain former employees and their beneficiaries." Under the proposed regulations, the Department of Labor would not have made individual determinations about whether any specific organizations or plans met these criteria but would have allowed the states to use the proposed guidelines to make those determinations. Thus, state insurance regulators would have had the authority to determine whether an employee benefit plan was a bona fide "collectively bargained" plan subject only to federal regulation or whether it was a MEWA, subject to state regulation.

Federal agencies propose thousands of regulations every year that, like these, generate little controversy and receive little or no media attention.[52] The proposed Department of Labor regulations did generate considerable response from "interested parties" who were invited by the Department to submit written comments on the proposed regulations. Some 47 "interested parties" did respond with written comments, many of them very detailed. Labor unions and law firms representing unions submitted the vast majority of these comments. All but a few expressed mild to strong opposition to the proposed regulations.

One of the most frequently expressed criticisms focused on

the ceding to state officials of the authority to determine the
ERISA status of union-sponsored health plans. These fears
were clearly voiced by the International Union of Bricklayers
& Allied Craftworkers:

To cede to 50 state agencies the power to decide whether a health
and welfare plan is a legitimate multiemployer plan, entitled to the
protection of ERISA, or a MEWA subject to state regulation is truly
to deliver multiemployer plans into the hands of what may chari-
tably be called at least their "potential" enemies. Regulatory agencies in a number of states are under the influence of rabidly anti-
union employer groups.[53]

Representatives of several labor organizations argued that the
new regulations would allow state insurance regulators to expand their dwindling jurisdiction. As one union official put it:

Although state insurance commissioners are supposed to ensure that
insurance companies are properly funded and protected, there is every incentive for state commissions to try to expand their reach over
collectively bargained plans that compete with the insurance companies generating revenue for the state treasury.[54]

Labor organizations were equally concerned about the requirement that 85 percent of each plan's participants had to be
regular members of the union. For them, this was clearly an
effort to limit unions' ability to expand by restricting the number of associate members they could sign up. The International
Union of Police Associations (IUPA) strongly defended what it
called the "associate member model plan":

The associate member model plan clearly was not restricted by Congress's 1983 MEWA amendments. Associate membership with full
and serious protection of membership rights is an avenue for
reform in the delivery of benefits to American working people. It
certainly does not represent a "bogus" insurance vehicle.[55]

The IUPA was but one of several law enforcement unions
that had expanded their rolls significantly by enrolling associate members. Another was the Virginia Beach Police Benevo-

lent Association Local No. 34, which offered its members health benefits through the Centurion Health Trust. Originally established to represent police officers in Virginia Beach and security guards at a local amusement park, in the early 1990s Local 34 had begun recruiting associate members across the country. Associate members were not required to be peace officers; membership was "open to anyone who supports law enforcement as a worthy goal." [56] Colorado regulators, who attempted to bar the union from soliciting members in their state, claimed that less than 1 percent of the plan's members were covered by a collective bargaining agreement and that 99 percent of the members "have no relationship with the union other than the health plan." [57]

One of the most thorough objections to the proposed rules regarding labor union health plans came from the AFL-CIO's National Coordinating Committee for Multiemployer Plans (NCCMP):

We believe that the Proposed Regulation would destroy many multi-employer plans—either as the result of erroneous determinations and harassment by states, or through the exhaustion of time, money, and effort necessary either to implement all the requirements of the Proposed Regulation or to defend a state's challenge. The NCCMP also fears that in an effort to comply with the technical requirements of the proposed Regulation and to avoid being deemed a MEWA by an overzealous state agency, many bona fide collectively bargained multiemployer plans will be required to terminate coverage for certain retirees and other employees and/or their dependents who, we believe, would be entitled to coverage under governing plan documents and applicable federal law.[58]

This statement appeared in the introduction to NCCMP's written response, which comprised some 45 pages in total. By contrast, the several letters received by the Department of Labor in support of the regulations were very brief. The National Association of Insurance Commissioners' letter, for example, was only three pages in length.

These written responses gave Department of Labor officials a clear indication of what they were up against. Despite a

clear need to fill the gaps in ERISA to stop sham unions from
marketing bogus health insurance plans, agency efforts would
meet with strong opposition from labor organizations and
only tepid support from state regulators and other groups. By
the fall of 1997, the Department of Labor had taken no action
on the regulations, which were still officially "under review"
by the agency.

CONCLUSIONS

One of the distinctive features of many white-collar crimes is
the role that law plays in their commission. When planning
armed robberies and burglaries, most criminals do not ready
teams of lawyers whose job includes delaying the police. Likewise, when confronted by police seeking their arrest, drug
dealers do not typically file civil suits challenging the legal authority of the police to intervene in their business affairs. Yet,
as we saw in earlier chapters, this is exactly what health insurance crooks have done. For them, ERISA has served as a tactical legal weapon, a resource to stall, delay, and frustrate regulators. An obvious first step in efforts to stop these criminals
is to neutralize their legal weapons. But as this chapter has
shown, achieving this obvious solution has not been easy.

If gaps existed in the criminal statutes defining crimes such
as armed robbery or burglary, legislators would move quickly
to fill those loopholes with little or no outside interference.
Few legitimate organizations would have an interest in delaying the revisions. But in the world of white-collar crime, a
blurry boundary exists between the interests of white-collar
criminals and those of legitimate business. When laws are
proposed to deal with white-collar crimes, legislators can en-
counter considerable outside interference from business groups
seeking to protect their privileges.

To take an example from outside the health care arena, in
the early 1980s, federal regulators at the Federal Home Loan
Bank Board (the principal regulators of thrifts) became aware

that reckless savings and loan owners were funding unsound and often illegal loans with huge amounts of money brought into their institutions through brokered deposits—large deposits often made by money managers for investment purposes. In 1984, those regulators sought changes in federal regulations that would have limited to $100,000 the amount that a single broker could place at any given thrift. Their efforts were met with scathing criticism from powerful groups within the financial community such as Merrill Lynch, which issued a report that "lambasted the proposed limitations on brokered deposits."[59] In similar fashion, business community members met the efforts of federal and state regulators to plug holes in ERISA with harsh criticism.

This chapter has also provided a window into the intricate dynamics of health care policy formation in the United States. In recent years, sociologists and other analysts have pointed to the increasingly prominent role that business groups play in the formulation of specific health care policies. Until the 1980s, health care policy was left largely in the hands of health care provider groups, including the American Medical Association and the American Hospital Association. Beginning in the early 1980s, however, as health care costs increased dramatically and as corporate profits declined as a result of a general restructuring of the economy, corporations began to play a much more active and often dominant role in health care policy debates.[60] One of the mechanisms corporate groups have used to influence policy has been "business health care coalitions" that "have served as forums for discussions and vehicles for collective action."[61] A principal form this collective action takes is the lobbying efforts by representatives of these coalitions to influence legislation.

In the foregoing discussion of the debates surrounding ERISA, the role that business health care coalitions played was significant. The ERISA Industry Council and the Self-Insurance Institute of America, for example, played major parts in defeating legislation that would have shifted regulatory authority over MEWAs to the states. These same groups strongly supported legislation that would have allowed MEWAS and association health plans to more easily escape state regulations. These actions were taken not because corporate heads were sympathetic to health insurance crooks, but because their own material interests were in keeping health care costs down by evading state regulations on their self-insured plans.

In discussions of health care policy generally, organized labor has not had as loud a voice as has corporate America. But on specific issues regarding ERISA health plans, its influence has been substantial. New regulations that would have prevented sham unions from marketing health insurance behind an ERISA shield were effectively killed by labor organizations, which saw in them a hidden threat to their autonomy and a potential limit on their ability to expand.

Finally, this chapter underscores the extent to which, at the end of the twentieth century, health care in the United States has become a commodity, to be bought, traded, and negotiated in the marketplace. Unlike other advanced countries where the minimum health care needs of citizens are guaranteed by the government, the private nature of medical care in the United States ensures that these kinds of debates over health care policy will be dominated by those groups with the most political and economic power. Ironically, those who are affected the most by these policies—the working men and women who must constantly worry about getting and keeping a job that will provide them and their families with adequate medical care—often have the faintest voices.

NOTES

1 Senate Committee on Labor and Human Resources, *Employer Group Purchasing Reform Act of 1995*, 104th Cong., 1st sess., 25 July 1995, 1.

2 Daniel Fox and Daniel Schaffer, "Health Policy and ERISA: Interest Groups and Semipreemption," *Journal of Health Politics, Policy and Law* 14 (1989): 242.

3 Quoted in ibid., 243.

4 House Select Committee on Aging, Subcommittee on Retirement Income and Employment, *Who's Minding Your Pension?* testimony of Patricia Ruth Donovan Petersen, Deputy Insurance Commissioner, State of Washington, 101st Cong., 1st sess., 15 November 1989, 289–90.

5 Senate Committee on Governmental Affairs, Permanent Subcommittee on Investigations, *Fraud and Abuse in Employer Sponsored Health Benefit Plans,* testimony of Jo Ann Howard, Texas State Board of Insurance, 101st Cong., 2d sess., 15 May 1990, 126.

6 House Select Committee on Aging, Subcommittee on Retirement Income and Employment, *Who's Minding Your Pension?* testimony of Raymond Maria, Acting Inspector General, U.S. Department of Labor, 101st Cong., 1st sess., 15 November 1989, 6.

7 Ibid., 7.

8 Senate Committee, *Fraud and Abuse in Employer Sponsored Health Benefit Plans,* 68.

9 General Accounting Office, *Employee Benefits: States Need Labor's Help Regulating Multiple Employer Welfare Arrangements,* GAO/HRD-92-40, March 1992, p. 2.

10 H.R. 2773, 102d Cong., 2d sess., 1991; H.R. 4919, 102d Cong., 2d sess., 1991; H.R. 5386, 102d Cong., 2d sess., 1991.

11 S. 2843, 102d Cong., 2d sess., 1991.

12 House Select Committee on Aging, Subcommittee on Retirement Income and Employment, *Small Business and Older Workers Health Benefits: Multiple Employer Welfare Arrangements, The Problem or the Solution,* testimony of James Kinder, Self-Insurance Institute of America, 102d Cong., 1st sess., 17 September 1991, 264.

13 House Committee on Education and Labor, Subcommittee on Labor-Management Relations, *Hearings on H.R. 2773, H.R. 4919, and H.R. 5386,* statement submitted by the AFL-CIO, 102d Cong., 2d sess., 16 June 1992, 153.

14 *MDPhysicians v. Wrotenberry,* 762 F. Supp. 695 (N.D. Tex. 1991).

15 *Atlantic Healthcare Benefits Trust v. Goggins,* 2 F.3d 1 (2d Cir. 1993).

16 Fla. Ins. Code § 624.438 (1994).

17 Creton Nelson-Morrill, "Florida MEWA Left 40,000 Bare," *National Underwriter,* 18 January 1993, p. 4.

18 Tex. Ins. Code ch. 21, subch. E.

19 Personal communication, Lee Jones, Texas Department of Insurance, 6 May 1997.

20 Senate Committee on Labor and Human Resources, testimony of Olena Berg, Assistant Secretary of Labor, 105th Cong., 2d sess., 1 October 1997.

21 797 F. Supp. 542, 545 (N.D. Tex. 1992).

22 U.S. Department of Labor, Pension and Welfare Benefits Administration, Opinions 91-17A, 92-04A, 92-05A, 92-07A, 93-29A(C).

23 Fla. Stat. tit. 32 § 468 (1991).

24 Tex. Labor Code tit. 2, ch. 91 (1993).

25 Bill Bowen, "Leasing Firms Slow to Apply for Licenses," *Dallas Business Journal,* 15 April 1994, p. 2.

26 Personal communication, Texas Department of Licensing and Registration, 1997.

27 H.R. 995, 104th Cong., 1st sess.

28 House Committee on Economic and Educational Opportunities, Subcommittee on Employer-Employee Relations, *Hearings on H.R. 995. The ERISA Targeted Health Insurance Reform Act,* 104th Cong., 1st sess., 10 March 1993.

29 Steven Brostoff, "Limited Bill Advances to House," *National Underwriter* (Life & Health/Financial Services ed.), 11 March 1996, p. 1.

30 Steve Langdom, "Kennedy, Kassebaum Steer Insurance Bill to Safety," *Congressional Quarterly,* 3 August 1996, 2197–2200.

31 House Committee on Education and the Workforce, Subcommittee on Employer-Employee Relations, *Hearings on H.R. 1515. The Expanded Portability and Health Insurance Coverage Act,* statement of Rep. Harris Fawell, 105th Cong., 1st sess., 8 May 1997, 3.

32 See, for example, House Committee, *Hearings on H.R. 1515,* statement of Cathy Hurwitt, Deputy Director, Citizen Action, 73–79.

33 House Committee, *Hearings on H.R. 995,* statement of Sean Sullivan, President, National Business Coalition on Health, 33.

34 "A Case of the MEWAs," *Washington Post,* 31 March 1997, p. A20.

35 Harris W. Fawell, "Squeezing Small Business," *Washington Post,* 16 April 1997, p. A17.

36 Ibid.

37 General Accounting Office, *Health Insurance Regulation: Variation in Recent State Small Employer Health Insurance,* GAO/HEHS-95-161FS, June 1995.

38 Ibid., 4.

39 Quoted in Robert Pear, "States Seek a Voice in Company Health Plans," *New York Times,* 1 December 1994, p. 28.

40 William Tucker, "Loopholes Hobble Health Coverage," *Insight Magazine,* 28 February 1994, p. 6.

41 The ERISA Industry Committee, *National Uniformity Brief #5* (Washington, D.C.: ERIC, 1997).

42 As quoted in Mary Jane Fischer, "Battle Royal Is Brewing Over ERISA Preemption," *National Underwriter* (Life/Health ed.), 10 April 1995, p. 17.

43 The right of ERISA plan sponsors to deny coverage was affirmed in 1992 when the Supreme Court refused to hear a case involving a Houston man who had been denied coverage for AIDS treatment. The plaintiff, John W. McGann, had sought reimbursement for treatment of his condition through the insurance plan provided by his employer, H&H Music. Soon thereafter, the company dropped its health insurance plan, enrolled its employees in a self-insured ERISA plan, and reduced the limit on McGann's coverage from $1 million to $5,000. McGann died the year before the Supreme Court's decision not to hear his case. Joan Biskupic, "AIDS Case Benefit Cut Let Stand," *Washington Post,* 10 November 1992, p. A1. The only recourse for a member of an ERISA plan who feels that he or she has been unfairly denied coverage is to appeal to the Department of Labor. But the Department's resources for handling these appeals are extremely thin; in 1992 it had only 31 staff members to handle some 180,000 complaints. National Association of Insurance Commissioners, "ERISA: A Call for Reform," 1994, p. 14.

44 Jon Gabel and Gail Jensen, "The Price of State Mandated Benefits," *Inquiry* 26 (1989): 419–31.

45 General Accounting Office, *Employer-Based Health Plans: Issues, Trends, and Challenges Posed by ERISA,* GAO/HEHS-95-167, July 1995, p. 22.

46 House Committee, *Hearings on H.R. 995,* statement of the National Association of Manufacturers, 24–25.

47 Ibid., 26.

48 Letter from Mark J. Ugoretz, President, ERISA Industry Committee, to Harris Fawell, 14 April 1997.

49 U.S. Department of Labor, Office of the Inspector General, *Semiannual Report to Congress, April 1–September 30, 1993* (Washington, D.C.: GPO, 1993), 42.

50 60 Fed. Reg. 39211 (1995) (to be codified at 29 C.F.R. § 2510).

51 Ibid.

52 A search of the Dow-Jones computerized databases that contain articles, reports, and other documents from thousands of newspapers, magazines, and trade periodicals located only two articles on the proposed regulations from the Department of Labor, both of which appeared in business trade periodicals.

53 Comments by John J. Flynn, Executive Vice President, International Union of Bricklayers & Allied Craftworkers, *Comments on Behalf of the International Union of Bricklayers and Allied Craftworkers, AFL-CIO, In Opposition to Proposed Regulation Under Section 3(40)*, 16 November 1995.

54 Kathleen M. Dowd, United Brotherhood of Carpenters and Joiners of America, *Comments of the United Brotherhood of Carpenters of America to Proposed Regulation Under Section 3(40) of ERISA*, 17 November 1995.

55 Michael T. Leibig and William Ford, *Comment on DOL Regulation of Employee Benefit Plans Pursuant to Collective Bargaining Agreements: The 29 U.S.C. 1002(40) Exception to MEWA Non-Preemption Rule*, 18 December 1995.

56 Douglas McLeod, "Regulators Seek to Bar Union Plan," *Business Insurance*, 27 March 1995, p. 1.

57 Stephen G. Smith, Assistant Attorney General, State of Colorado, *Proposed Regulation for Plans Established or Maintained Pursuant to Collective Bargaining Agreements Under 3(40)(A)*, 31 October 1995.

58 National Coordinating Committee for Multiemployer Plans, *Comments to Proposed Regulation Under Section 3(40) of ERISA*, 18 December 1995, p. 2.

59 Kitty Calavita, Henry Pontell, and Robert Tillman, *Big Money Crime: Fraud and Politics in the Savings and Loan Crisis* (Berkeley: University of California Press, 1997), 95.

60 Allen Imershein, Philip Rond, and Mary Mathis, "Restructuring Patterns of Elite Dominance and the Formation of State Policy in Health Care," *American Journal of Sociology* 97 (1992): 970–93.

61 Beth Mintz, "Business Participation in Health Care Policy Reform: Factors Contributing to Collective Action Within the Business Community," *Social Problems* 42 (1995): 412.

Conclusions

B
Y the fall of 1997, much had changed since the early years of the decade when William Loeb and Lawernce Kenemore were able to defraud thousands of working Americans out of millions of dollars with empty promises of affordable health insurance. In 1996, Congress approved and President Clinton signed into law the Kennedy-Kassebaum Act, which guaranteed that workers would not lose their medical coverage when they changed jobs and limited the use of preexisting conditions in denying applicants medical coverage.[1] The Tax Reform Act of 1997 implemented a schedule in which the self-employed could deduct a portion of their health insurance costs from their taxes, increasing to 80 percent by the year 2006.[2] As we saw in the last chapter, a number of states enacted small group reform measures that sought to make affordable health insurance more available to small business employees. In addition, many states passed laws giving their departments of insurance limited regulatory powers over MEWAs and other employee benefit plans.

These measures, combined with more aggressive enforcement efforts by the Department of Labor, had a positive effect in reducing the incidence of small business health insurance fraud.[3] Available statistical information and the comments

made by regulators and law enforcement agents interviewed
for this study indicate that, after peaking somewhere in 1992–
1993, the number of bogus MEWAs, fraudulent employee leasing companies, and sham unions in operation began to decline.[4] The problem has not disappeared, but the blatant kinds
of nationwide health insurance scams run by people like Loeb
and Kenemore started to show up less frequently.

At the same time, many of the conditions that gave rise to
the wave of health insurance frauds in the late 1980s and early
1990s remained stubbornly entrenched. Despite the efforts of
individual states to make health insurance more available, an
increasing number of Americans were living without it. In
1988, some 15.2 percent of the population under age 65 did
not have health insurance coverage; by 1995, that proportion
had increased to 17.4 percent. Even more discouraging was the
fact that similar increases occurred in those states where small
group reform policies had been implemented. In California, the
proportion of those uninsured increased from 20 percent to
22.7 percent, and in Texas, the proportion increased from 26
percent to 27 percent.[5] Federal laws clearly delineating the
regulatory authority of the states and federal agencies over
MEWAs and labor unions had not been enacted, and, as we saw
in the preceding chapter, there was a move afoot in Congress
to reverse the gains made by states in regulating MEWAs.

Thus, despite the fact that significant gains had been made
in the fight against small business health insurance fraud, the
basic sources of the problem remained in place: unmet demand for medical benefits by self-employed and small business
employees and ambiguous laws regarding the regulation of
ERISA health plans.

Monetary losses from health insurance scams involving
MEWAs or bogus labor unions constitute a small portion of the
$100 billion lost every year to fraud and abuse in the health
care system. Nonetheless, the complex nature of this form of
fraud and its stubborn resistance to efforts to eliminate it raise
important issues for our understanding of the origins and consequences of white-collar crime.

HEALTH INSURANCE FRAUD
AS ORGANIZED CRIME

In the public's mind, there is a sharp distinction between the people involved in organized crime and those involved in white-collar crime. The phrase *organized crime* conjures up images—derived mostly from Hollywood movies—of broad-shouldered henchmen wearing long overcoats, black shirts and white ties and speaking a vernacular that includes pronouns such as "dese," "dem," and "dose." The public's image of the white-collar criminal is likely that of a distinguished looking middle-aged white male, wearing a pin-striped suit and speaking in the mannered tones of an Ivy League school graduate.

Likewise, in traditional criminological thinking, organized crime groups and white-collar criminals are distinguished by differences in their organization, goals, and methods. In the older criminological view, organized crime groups were formed primarily for the purpose of monetary gain through the commission of illegal acts on an ongoing basis, their membership was restricted to males of certain ethnic backgrounds, and violence (either executed or implied) was a central element of their illegal activities. White-collar criminals, by contrast, were individuals employed in organizations whose primary goals were legitimate, who committed the illegal acts of deception and fraud but not violence.

In recent years, several prominent criminologists have challenged this traditional distinction between organized crime and white-collar crime. Kitty Calavita and Henry Pontell have argued that organized crime and white-collar crime may have much more in common than was previously believed. They state that individuals in corporate contexts are engaged in organized crime if "(1) the purpose of the corporation or company is primarily to provide a vehicle for the production of illegal activity for personal gain and (2) the crimes are premeditated, organized, continuous, and facilitated by the participation of public officials."[6] Given this definition, the networks of savings and loan executives who committed numerous financial crimes at thrifts across the country and who used their political influence to clear the way for their illegal activities would qualify as members of organized crime groups.

Similarly, the crimes described in this book were not carried out by individual offenders operating in isolation but were perpetrated by organized networks of individuals and organizations who operate what essentially are ongoing criminal enterprises, whose form may change but whose illicit goals remain the same. Looking at the series of interconnected schemes described in Chapter 4 that began with William Loeb, one is struck by the high degree of organization that was required to coordinate the activities of numerous individuals operating in different parts of the country over long periods of time, all of whom utilized the same basic strategy to perpetrate their crimes. In addition to the principals, who often served as trustees for the so-called union trust funds, these schemes employed legions of brokers and agents to set up, market, and collect premiums for the health insurance plans, as well as lawyers and accountants to fend off and deceive regulators. To be fair, not all of these individuals were aware that they were participating in illegal schemes. Nonetheless, witting or unwitting, they were part of a large-scale, organized effort to generate profits through illegal activities. Also striking is the way in which these criminal networks were able to continue despite the incarceration of several of their founding members, also true in traditional organized crime groups. This suggests that these were truly crimes of organizations, not simply of individuals.

Far from a radical view espoused by academics, a number of prominent law enforcement officials have advocated this new definition of organized crime. The former Inspector General for the Department of Labor, Julian De La Rosa, testified before a congressional committee in 1991 regarding the jurisdiction of the Office of Labor Racketeering (OLR):

I want to go on record today as opposing such a narrow construction of "organized crime" and, by extension, OLR's authority. Labor racketeering today is not the province of any particular ethnic subgroup and, in the health and welfare field, labor racketeering activities impact upon all employees, not just those employees who are parties to collective bargaining agreements. OLR's current focus is on criminal "enterprises" rather than organized crime "families."[7]

A similar understanding of organized crime has been advocated by De La Rosa's successor, Charles Masten. In a statement before the House Appropriations Committee, Masten explained some of the newer areas of investigation the agency was undertaking:

Over the past few years, we have seen a significant increase in labor racketeering activities by nontraditional organized crime groups (e.g., Russian, Asian, etc.) and by a new generation of "white-collar racketeers" such as lawyers, accountants, and brokers who utilize complex financial schemes to defraud the public. In particular, we have seen an increase in the activities of these nontraditional criminal elements in the employee benefit plan area.[8]

De La Rosa's and Masten's comments indicate an awareness of the need to understand the organizational roots and legal complexities of white-collar crimes such as those committed in the health benefits field.

The line between traditional organized crime groups and white-collar criminals has become even more blurred in recent years as Mafia-run organizations have branched out into new territories. In 1996, for example, New Jersey law enforcement officials revealed a scheme involving a number of alleged members and associates of the Genovese crime family who took over a New Jersey company, Tri-Con, that "managed group medical, dental and optical programs for employers and unions with networks of health-care providers."[9] The firm's officers allegedly extorted kickbacks, skimmed money from clients, and assisted providers in submitting false claims. The organization had its official headquarters in offices in northern New Jersey but was actually operated out of two social clubs by alleged mob associates. Tri-Con's chief economic officer was a former New Jersey police officer who had served ten years in prison for armed robbery, extortion, and racketeering.[10]

Law enforcement officials say that the Tri-Con case may be indicative of an emerging trend in which traditional organized crime groups are starting to move into the lucrative health care industry. According to some experts, law enforcement's relentless pressure on the Mafia over the past couple of decades has forced the group out of its traditional economic strongholds: the construction industry, garbage hauling cartels, and control of food and produce markets. As a result, the organized crime group has turned to white-collar crime. As one FBI official put it, "They are analogous to companies in Chapter 11 bankruptcy. They are still in business but many of their old moneymaking bases have dried up and they are moving into new industries to fill the cash void."[11]

Another one of these new industries that the Mafia has recently discovered is the securities industry. In the fall of 1997, the U.S. Attorney in Brooklyn, New York, indicted several high-ranking members of the Genovese and Bonano crime families on charges that they conspired with officials at a Wall Street brokerage firm to manipulate stock prices of a company that operated health clubs.[12] In a related case, federal prosecutors charged members of the Gambino family with inflating stock prices by rewarding brokers who agreed to sell shares to their clients with bags of marijuana and punishing a rival firm's representative who threatened to expose the scheme by dangling him out the window of a ninth-floor office.[13] Wall Street remains an attractive target for mobsters honing their white-collar criminal skills.

HEALTH INSURANCE FRAUD
AS VIOLENT CRIME

The traditional assumption that white-collar crimes were nonviolent came into question in the 1960s by academics and consumer advocates who started referring to workplace safety violations, acts of environmental destruction, and the manufacture of unsafe products as *corporate violence*. One of the early advocates of this perspective was social activist Ralph Nader who, in 1967, wrote: "The harm done to health and safety by business crime should dispel the distinguishing characteristic of 'white-collar crime' as being the absence of physical threat." [14] He would later refer to acts of environmental pollution and the exposure of employees to hazardous working conditions as "postponed violence" because the harmful consequences of these acts may not appear for many years. [15] By the 1980s, the concept of corporate violence was firmly established in the academic literature on white-collar crime, and case studies began appearing that described instances of environmental destruction and death and injury in the workplace as routine by-products of the corporate pursuit of profit. [16]

Important as these studies have been in expanding our definition of violence, they focus almost exclusively on organizations and individuals involved in industrial and manufacturing enterprises. White-collar crimes occurring in financial industries are still generally regarded as nonviolent. Yet health insurance frauds of the sort described in this book are good examples of crimes that originate "on paper" (that is, in the writing of health insurance policies and the collection of premiums) whose purpose is monetary gain, but whose ultimate *consequences* may include serious physical harm, including death, to their victims. Labeling these crimes as nonviolent minimizes these harms.

The preceding chapters have described the plights of numerous victims of health insurance schemes who, after realizing their insurance policies were worthless, were unable to obtain medical care and whose physical conditions worsened as a result. Louise Rayfield (Introduction), ripped off in a Loeb scheme, was unable to obtain a cornea transplant and was forced to live with blurred vision for the rest of her life. Janet Parker, a Rubell-Helm victim (Chapter 2), was unable to provide her son with needed treatments for his asthma attacks.

Mary Lee Johnson, the nurse in Missouri whose employer made the mistake of buying a health insurance policy from Lawernce Kenemore (Chapter 5), lost the use of her leg when she was unable to afford treatments by a specialist. All of these people suffered physical harm to the same degree as many victims of armed robberies and assaults do as a result of their victimization by white-collar criminals. For these reasons, health insurance fraud should be considered violent crime.

There are some differences, of course, in this form of white-collar violence and the violence surrounding more traditional types of crime. Barbara Chasin distinguishes *interpersonal violence* from *structural violence*:

Interpersonal violence is what many experts and most of us mean when we use the word [*violence*]—identifiable persons injure others and are usually aware that they have done so. Structural violence, on the other hand, is a consequence of the routine workings of a society, especially of its stratification system. Structural violence usually occurs when people's lives are made demonstrably worse by their lack of access to resources.

Victims of structural violence do not see and generally are unaware of those responsible for their injuries, while those responsible rarely see the suffering their actions have caused.

Interpersonal violence occurs most frequently among people of the same economic group and often members of the same community or household. Structural violence, on the other hand, is a direct or indirect result of decisions made at the elite level of society—those who suffer are from less privileged groups.[17]

By this definition, Louise Rayfield, Janet Parker's son, and Mary Lee Johnson were all victims of structural violence. They were members of less privileged groups whose lives were made "demonstrably worse by their lack of access to resources," and who suffered physical harm as a result of the acts of individuals who "rarely see the suffering their actions have caused."

The American media and many of our politicians are currently fixated on interpersonal violence. Television programs and movies sensationalize gory acts of brutality, while politicians give rousing speeches about "getting tough on crime" and the need to lock up more criminals. Yet this focus tends to eclipse the more mundane acts of structural violence that occur around us every day. It prevents us from recognizing the serious harm these acts of structural violence inflict on individuals. Members of Congress, who are quick to decry violence by inner-city youths, must broaden their horizons to appreciate the serious physical consequences of health insurance fraud and be more energetic in their attempts to stop the problem at its source. Their inaction suggests more concern with the interests of large corporations than with the suffering of individuals.

WHITE-COLLAR CRIME IN A GLOBAL ECONOMY

Health insurance fraud is but one of several financial crimes involving employee benefits. White-collar criminals are like the famous bank robber Willie Sutton who, when asked why he robbed banks, said "because that's where the money is." Likewise, white-collar racketeers are drawn to areas where large amounts of money accumulate and where funds can be moved rapidly from one place to another with little regulatory oversight or accountability. White-collar thieves who steal through health insurance scams are just as likely to operate illegal schemes involving workers' compensation premiums or pension funds. Crime in both of these areas, in fact, is growing at alarming rates.[18] All types of health insurance fraud are emblematic of the emerging forms of white-collar crime that reflect the changing economy of the late twentieth century.

The massive changes currently taking place in the economy and the workplace are too broad to describe in any detail here, but we can mention some of the ways these changes are making the situation of workers much more precarious and making them much more vulnerable to fraud and abuse. Today, many American workers who seek security in medical and retirement benefits find themselves virtually abandoned by both the government and private industry. On the one hand, employers tell their employees that to compete in the global marketplace they can no longer afford to pay such "luxuries" as health and retirement benefits, or even to promise a steady job. On the other hand, the American government, particularly Republican congressional leaders, exhort workers to stop looking to the government to take care of their basic needs and urge them to become more self-sufficient. The results are evident in statistics on employment benefits. In 1979, 48 percent of American workers between the ages of 18 and 64, employed in the private sector, received some type of pension benefits. By 1993, that proportion had declined to 45 percent. In that same period, the proportion of private-sector workers receiving some type of health benefits declined from 71 to 64 percent.[19] In this environment, stories abound of people taking low-paying jobs that barely provide a subsistent existence to obtain health benefits.

These trends are not having the same impact on all workers. Another aspect of the restructuring of the American economy is a growing disparity in the material position of those at the top and those at the bottom of the occupational ladder. Those at the top are individuals employed as what former Secretary of Labor Robert Reich calls "symbolic analysts"—computer programmers, attorneys, bankers, and Wall Street analysts. These workers are becoming increasingly prosperous as they benefit from the shift to an information-based economy.[20] Those at the bottom—poorly educated, low-skilled, and low-paid workers employed in places such as restaurants, garages, grocery stores, and construction companies— are finding their situations eroding fast as their wages decline, their job security evaporates, and the cost of living rises. As part of this general erosion of their position, people at the bottom find themselves increasingly at risk of being ripped off in the kinds of scams that have been described in this book. Yet, as was mentioned in Chapter 3, highly educated professionals may also find themselves vulnerable to these frauds as the logic of "outsourcing" works its way up the occupational ladder.

At the same time that American workers' more precarious situations make them easier targets for employee benefit scams, changes in the technological infrastructure of financial industries make it easier for white-collar criminals to set up and operate their illegal schemes. The rapid diffusion of computer technology into all aspects of business and commerce has been a prime factor behind the movement toward a global economy. Nowhere has the impact of this technological revolution been more evident than in the financial industries, including banking and insurance. The very nature of the insurance industry, with a minimum reliance on face-to-face contacts between agents and clients and an emphasis on claims processing procedures that are largely automated, has allowed it to become "the most highly automated white-collar industry."[21] As a result of this transformation, the basic work of the insurance industry—traditionally done on paper in the form of actuarial analyses, claims processing, and so on—is now carried out on computers, and there is no longer any need for a physical, central office located in proximity to the clients. Instead, insurance companies' work has become highly decentralized and mobile, and a company's various offices may be located in different parts of the country and even the world.

This mobility and decentralization of operations is ideal for sophisticated white-collar criminals who commit what Chapter 4 calls recombinant fraud. White-collar criminals, equipped with sophisticated computerized data processing and communications technology, are able to set up highly mobile operations that do business nationally and internationally and whose only geographical ties may be a post office box where premium checks are collected. When insurance regulators or law enforcement officials close in on the illegal operation, the operators can quickly move it to another state (often assuming a new organizational identity) with little or no disruption to their billing and premium collections. For example, within several months after California regulators shut down Lawernce Kenemore's insurance agency, Bestland, he was marketing a combined health insurance/workers' compensation plan nationwide under the auspices of Association of Trust and Guarantee (ATG), headquartered in Texas. According to federal prosecutors, when state regulators attempted to close down ATG:

> [Kenemore] engaged in a shell game with regulators by dropping ATG's original name (ATG Association of Trust and Guarantee) and adopting a multiplicity of new business names, including ATG Associations (A Trust), Utah ATG (A Trust), North Carolina ATG (A Trust), and other names using the acronym "ATG.". . . In January of 1994, Kenemore publicly boasted at a training program for ATG's sales force of his ability to evade state regulation by setting up new unions and new versions of ATG: "I can set them up faster than they can close them down."[22]

Kenemore's strategy typifies the basic elements of recombinant fraud in which organizations are constantly being created, shut down, and recreated in an ongoing response to the obstacles presented by law enforcement officials and regulators. As one investigator put it:

> State borders mean nothing to these swindlers. They pull their cons, sell a few thousand policies, collect a few million dollars and when the heat builds up they slither to the next state and start again.[23]

In these schemes, organizations are used as weapons by white-collar criminals in the same way that bank robbers use guns to carry out their crimes.[24]

IMPACT OF DEREGULATION

The Introduction discusses how the small business health insurance industry has been transformed into a criminogenic industry. A key factor in this transformation was the de facto deregulation of a segment of that industry by the Employee

Retirement Income Security Act (ERISA). While ERISA's original sponsors implied that state regulation would be replaced by federal regulation, the subsequent absence of any meaningful federal oversight of ERISA plans meant that those plans operated effectively outside of the regulations faced by insurance companies. Like the proponents of the deregulation of the thrift industry in the early 1980s, current supporters of the continued deregulation of ERISA plans argue for the needs of plan sponsors to remain flexible and free to innovate without the cumbersome burdens of government regulations.

This push to deregulate the health insurance and the savings and loan industries is part of a larger movement to deregulate financial industries generally in the emerging global economy. Only months after the last failed savings and loan was put to rest, for example, the banking industry was pressing Washington to repeal the Glass-Steagall Act of 1933, which prevented commercial banks from marketing securities, arguing that the law severely limited their ability to compete on the global market with foreign banks that faced no such restrictions. Several analysts have identified this push to deregulate as a key element in the globalization of the world's markets:

The rise of global financial markets makes it increasingly difficult for national governments to formulate economic policy, much less enforce it. In the increasingly anarchic world of high-speed money, the dilemma facing national political leaders is clear. Impose regulations, and sit back and watch how quickly financial institutions slip out from under them by changing their looks, disappearing into other corporations, or otherwise rearranging their affairs to make life difficult for regulators. At the same time, bankers argue that to the extent the regulations are observed, they pose a handicap to international competition. Yet the history of deregulation is littered with scandals and financial foolishness for which a handful of banks, but mostly millions of taxpayers and depositors, have paid a heavy price.[25]

Inevitably, deregulated money in a global economy finds its way into offshore havens where it becomes a resource for a new breed of international criminals:

Big money hides itself in the global economy. Respectable capital mingles alongside dirty money from illegal enterprise (drugs, gambling, illicit arms sales) because the offshore banking centers allow both to hide from the same things: national taxation and the surveillance of government regulators.[26]

These trends are part of larger political contests, "commonly described as deregulation," in which capital seeks to escape from government regulation.[27]

Offshore insurance companies played a prominent role in many of the health insurance scams described here. Operators of these bogus MEWAS and union-sponsored plans would claim to be fully or partially insured by companies headquartered in countries like the Cayman Islands, the Turks and Caicos Islands, and Antigua—countries where regulation is lax and information on the health of financial institutions is hard to come by. While the insurance provided by these offshore companies would often prove to be practically worthless, making that determination would often take stateside regulators operating with very limited budgets months and even years. Even when regulators succeeded in determining that an offshore company was unstable or fraudulent, this did little to slow down the crooks. For example, in a four-year period, the operators of Consolidated Local 867 and its successor the National Council of Allied Employees (NCAE) sold health insurance policies they claimed were backed by a succession of no less than six offshore insurance companies, all of which were domiciled in the Caribbean and would later be classified as "unacceptable" by California regulators. The regulators' determinations were of little consequence to William Loeb and his fellow promoters; all they had to do when one insurer was prohibited from doing business in California was to roll over their policyholders into a new plan offered by another offshore insurer, until that firm was eventually barred from doing business in the state.

The original idea behind MEWAS and other health insurance "trusts" was that they would be local in nature, operated by trade associations, local union officials, or groups of employers in a community that would pool their resources to benefit employees. The sponsors of ERISA could not have foreseen how these local organizations would become part of the largely unregulated flow of capital around the world. Nor could they have foreseen how workers in states such as California, Texas, or Florida, who thought they were simply setting money aside to pay for future medical needs, could so easily get caught up in what are essentially international money laundering schemes. The plight of these workers is but one more piece of evidence attesting to the "down side" of the new global economy.

HEALTH CARE AND THE MARKETPLACE

As this book was being written, the country was engaged in a nationwide debate on health care reform. Skyrocketing medical costs and growing numbers of uninsured residents (who often go unnoticed until they show up in emergency rooms) convinced many that America is facing a health care crisis. At the root of this debate is the question over who should pay for the costs of health care. This issue, while present in past health care debates, has taken on more significance in recent years as health care costs have been driven upward by changes in the population: a growing number of elderly patients with chronic conditions that require lengthy and expensive treatments and a declining proportion of young healthy people to pay these costs. Should these mounting costs be borne by individuals who "invest" in their own health care by taking out private insurance or medical savings accounts? Or should these costs be spread out over society as a whole, with the wealthier members of society required to pay for far more than their own individual health care needs and the poorer members required to pay for a relatively small portion of their health care costs? At the level of policy, should health care be distributed by for-profit private entities that operate in a marketplace? Or should some minimal standard of health care be provided by the government?

Those who argue for allowing the invisible hand of the marketplace to determine who shall receive medical care and how much they shall receive see the issue primarily in economic terms. For them, the marketplace for health care is just like any other with a limited supply and a potentially infinite demand for services. From this perspective, the basic question is how to maximize efficiency both on the part of producers— for example, physicians, hospitals, and clinics—and on the part of consumers. Efficiency on the part of producers is best obtained through "managed competition"—health maintenance and similar organizations—that compete for customers by lowering their costs and discouraging waste and unnecessary treatments on the part of providers. Consumer efficiency is enhanced through mechanisms such as copayments that discourage the overutilization of health care services. Under the conditions of the marketplace, the argument continues, consumers' health is actually promoted by giving them economic incentives to engage in healthy behavior rather than unhealthy behavior, as, for example, when smokers are required to pay more for health insurance.

The critics of this position assert that health care is not just another market and therefore should not be left to the marketplace:

On the supply side, the health industry violates several conditions of a free market. Unlike the supermarket business, there is not "free entry." You cannot simply open a hospital, or hang out your shingle as a doctor. This gives health-care providers a degree of market power that compromises the competitive model—and raises prices. On the demand side, consumers lack the special knowledge to shop for a doctor the way they buy a car, and lack a perfectly free choice of health-insurer.[28]

More than simply violating economic assumptions, health care services are fundamentally different from those provided by other industries. Consumers can rationally decide not to purchase a new automobile or take a vacation without suffering any serious harm. And society does not feel a moral obligation to ensure that all its members have access to a new car or a vacation. By contrast, persons confronting a situation where they know that they must have a surgical procedure or face life threatening or debilitating consequences cannot simply put it off until the price becomes more affordable. Moreover, as a society we find it difficult to stand by and watch others suffer the consequences of being unable to purchase medical treatments. Critics of the market approach recognize that there does not exist an unlimited supply of medical care and there therefore must be some mechanism for rationing these services. But they also recognize society's moral obligation to do all it can to ensure the well-being of its members. Thus, some form of government intervention in the health care marketplace is necessary to prevent our society from splitting into two basic groups: employees of large organizations that can fund relatively inexpensive group insurance policies thereby guaranteeing their employees ready access to advanced medical care, and an underclass of workers who, because of their medical histories or the size of their employers, are considered "undesirable" by insurance companies and who find themselves effectively barred from obtaining all but the most minimal levels of health care.

Health insurance frauds of the sort described in this book are part of this larger debate on health care. As noted earlier, the most fundamental problem stems from persistent unmet demand for medical benefits by large segments of the population who have fallen between the cracks of both public and private health insurance programs. Many of these people are part of the so-called working poor, individuals who are not poor enough to qualify for welfare and Medicaid, but who do not earn enough money to afford either group or individual health policies from private insurance companies. For these people, the health care marketplace is clearly not working.

LOOKING AHEAD

Yet, as 1997 came to a close, there were glimmers of hope. The federal budget approved in the summer of 1997 set aside $24 billion, funded in part by new taxes levied on cigarettes, to be used by states to provide health insurance to uninsured children.[29] And the Clinton administration had begun looking into ways to provide health insurance to another group in dire need of insurance: the estimated 3 million Americans between the ages of 55 and 64 who have lost their medical benefits through retirement or corporate downsizing but who are too young to qualify for Medicare.[30]

These measures, while laudable, are piecemeal and their outcomes uncertain. The children's insurance plan, for example, would provide insurance to fewer than 2.5 million of the country's 10 million uninsured children.[31] Even with these programs in place, millions of American workers will still be desperate for health insurance for themselves and their families and susceptible to fraudulent schemes that take advantage of their difficult circumstances. A lasting solution to the problem of health insurance fraud can be secured only if we, as a nation, find the will to ensure adequate medical care for all Americans.

NOTES

1 Steve Langdom, "Kennedy, Kassebaum Steer Insurance Bill to Safety," *Congressional Quarterly*, 3 August 1996, p. 2198.

2 John Harris and Eric Pianin, "Bipartisanship Reigns at Budget Signing," *Washington Post*, 6 August 1997, p. A1.

3 In the early 1990s, the Department of Labor's Office of Labor Racketeering (OLR) made health insurance fraud a priority and began an aggressive campaign to investigate and prosecute fraud among ERISA health plans. By the fall of 1993, OLR reported having closed 17 cases involving bogus health plans that, together, operated in 48 states and left some 127,000 victims with $110,407,000 in unpaid medical bills. These 17

cases produced 55 indictments, 42 convictions, and fines and restitutions totaling over $52 million. U.S. Department of Labor, Office of the Inspector General, *Semiannual Report to Congress, April 1–Sept. 30, 1993* (Washington, D.C.: GPO, 1993), 41. In March 1994, the Secretary of Labor, Robert Reich, held a press conference announcing a "crackdown" on MEWA fraud, beginning with court actions taken within the week to close five bogus health insurance plans—including Local 211 in Texas. Albert Karr, "U.S. Acts Against Health Insurance Firms," *Wall Street Journal,* 1 April 1994, p. B2.

4 For a fuller description of these data, see Robert Tillman, "Controlling Fraud in the Small Business Health Insurance Industry," final report to the National Institute of Justice, 1998.

5 General Accounting Office, *A Profile of the Uninsured in Selected States,* GAO/HRD-91-31FS, February 1991; Employee Benefit Research Institute, *Sources of Health Insurance and Characteristics of the Uninsured* (Washington, D.C.: Employee Benefit Research Institute, 1996).

6 Kitty Calavita and Henry Pontell, "Savings and Loan Fraud as Organized Crime: Toward a Conceptual Typology of Corporate Illegality," *Criminology* 31 (1993): 529.

7 House Select Committee on Aging, Subcommittee on Retirement Income and Employment, *Small Business and Older Workers Health Benefits: Multiple Employer Welfare Arrangements, The Problem or the Solution,* 102d Cong., 1st sess., 17 September 1991, 70–84.

8 House Committee on Appropriations, Subcommittee on Labor, Health and Human Services, Education and Related Agencies, statement of Charles Masten, 105th Cong., 1st sess., 10 April 1997.

9 Selwyn Raab, "New Jersey Officials Say Mafia Infiltrated Health-Care Industry," *New York Times,* 22 August 1996, p. B-5.

10 Ibid.; Douglas McLeod, "N.J. Probing Health Plan's Mob Ties," *Business Insurance,* 26 August 1996, p. 1.

11 Selwyn Raab, "Officials Say Mob Is Shifting Crime to New Industries," *New York Times,* 10 February 1997, p. A-1.

12 Benjamin Weiser, "Brokers and Mob Linked in Swindle," *New York Times,* 26 November 1997, p. 1A.

13 Michael Schroeder, "U.S. Accuses 13 of Stock Fraud with Links to Organized Crime," *Wall Street Journal,* 14 November 1997, p. B19.

14 Ralph Nader, "Business Crime," *New Republic,* 1 July 1967, p. 7.

15 Quoted in Alex Thio, *Deviant Behavior,* 3d ed. (New York: Harper and Row, 1988), 424.

16 Stuart Hills, *Corporate Violence* (Totawa, N.J.: Rowan and Littlefield, 1987); Russell Mokhiber, *Corporate Crime and Violence* (San Francisco:

Sierra Club Books, 1988); Nancy Frank and Michael Lynch, *Corporate Crime, Corporate Violence* (Albany, N.Y.: Harrow and Heston, 1992).

17 Barbara Chasin, *Inequality and Violence in the United States* (Atlantic Heights, N.J.: Humanities Press, 1997), 4.

18 John Greenwald, "Is Your 401(k) at Risk?" *Time,* 11 December 1995, p. 66; Ellen Schultze, "Some Workers Find Retirement Nest Eggs Full of Strange Assets," *Wall Street Journal,* 5 June 1995, p. 1; John McKinnon, "Officials Plan Fraud Probe in Workers' Comp Market," *Wall Street Journal,* 4 June 1997, p. B2.

19 These data are for private-sector wage and salary workers between the ages of 18 and 64 with at least 20 weekly hours and 26 weeks of work. Lawrence Mishel, Jared Bernstein, and John Schmitt, *The State of Working America 1996–97* (Washington: Economic Policy Institute, 1997).

20 Robert Reich, *The Work of Nations* (New York: Vintage, 1991).

21 Manuel Castells, *The Informational City* (Oxford: Blackwell, 1989), 160.

22 *Reich v. Kenemore,* No. 3-95-CV-0105-R (N.D. Tex. 1995) ("Plaintiff's Memorandum in Support of Application for Temporary Restraining Order, Order to Show Cause, and Preliminary Injunction," 11).

23 Quoted in Andrew Schneider and Doug Sword, "Victims of Empty Promises," *Times Union* (Albany, N.Y.), 12 February 1995, p. A-3.

24 Stanton Wheeler and Mitchell Rothman, "The Organization as Weapon in White Collar Crime," *Michigan Law Review* 80 (1982): 1403–26.

25 Richard Barnet and John Cavanagh, *Global Dreams: Imperial Corporations and the New World Order* (New York: Touchstone, 1994), 397.

26 William Greider, *One World, Ready or Not: The Manic Logic of Global Capitalism* (New York: Simon & Schuster, 1997), 33.

27 Ibid.

28 Robert Kuttner, *Everything for Sale: The Virtues and Limits of Markets* (New York: Knopf, 1997), 17–18.

29 Robert Pear, "$24 Billion to Be Set Aside for Children's Medical Care," *New York Times,* 30 July 1997, p. A17.

30 Julia Lawlor, "Between Work and Medicare, a Health Gap," *New York Times,* 28 December 1997, p. 1A.

31 Pear, "$24 Billion."

Index